# The *Wisdom* of Weddings

*Life Lessons from That Special Day*

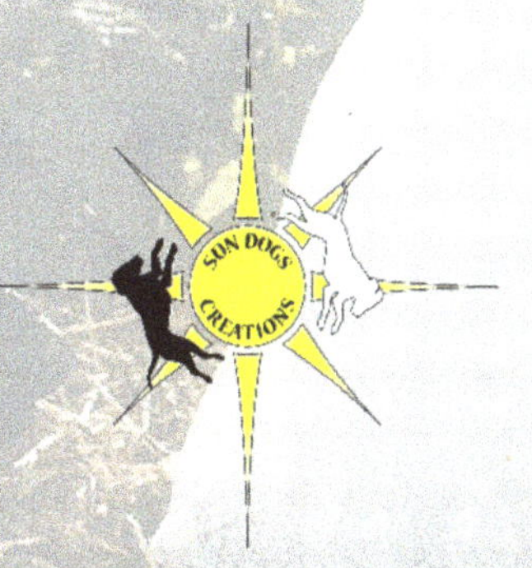

## LAINE CUNNINGHAM

The Wisdom of Weddings
Life Lessons from That Special Day

Published by Sun Dogs Creations
*Changing the World One Book at a Time*
ISBN: 9781946732514

Softcover Edition

Cover Design by Angel Leya

# *Introduction*

Weddings are as unique as the couple reciting their vows. Weddings can be imbued with religious elements or can be carried out as official affairs. The ceremony might last for minutes or hours. The event can take place at a tropical beach paradise, in a glittery Las Vegas chapel, or during a festival like Burning Man.

Some couples will begin their marriages in ways that are far from common. They might elope, perform a Pagan handfasting, share their vows alongside another couple in a double wedding, or relive their special day by renewing their vows.

No matter what type of wedding takes place, the excitement sparked by this singularly important milestone is always carried on waves of joy. The day marks a new beginning, one in which two individuals will merge their ideas, their efforts, and their love. Together they will move forward into a new life, one that resonates with the presence of the other.

The profound meaning of this single day is never-ending. The insights gained during the preparations, the shared joy, and the whirlwind of delight can imbue our lives with heartfelt passion. Our days become happier with *The Wisdom of Weddings*, and our hearts grow big enough to envelop the world.

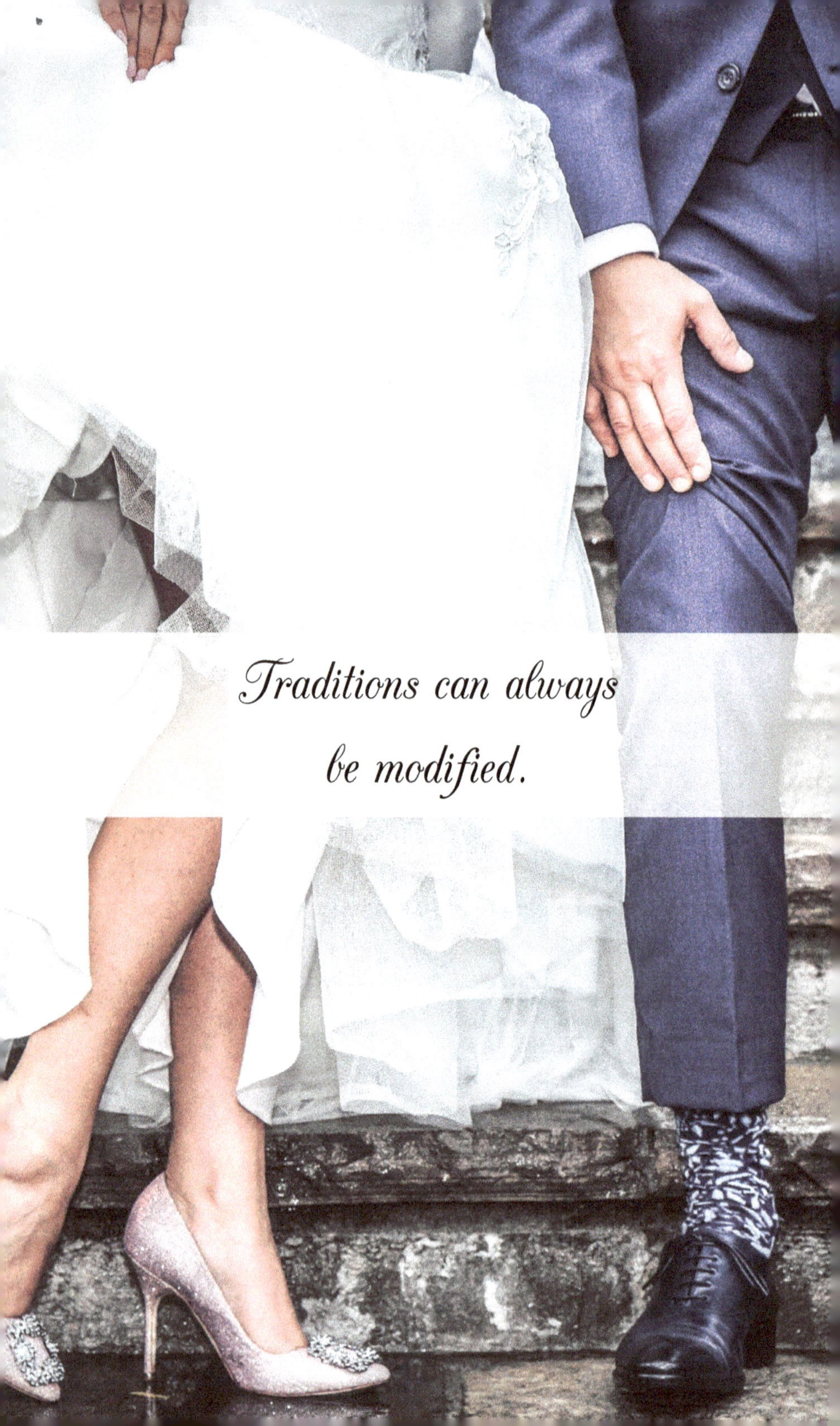

Traditions can always
be modified.

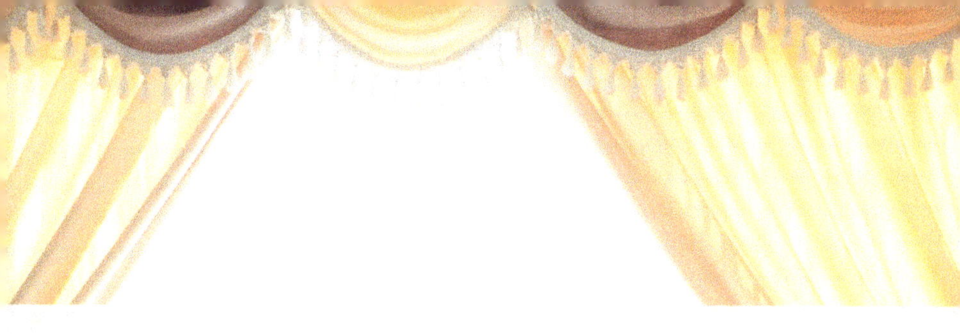

A beautiful outfit cannot outshine

the beauty within.

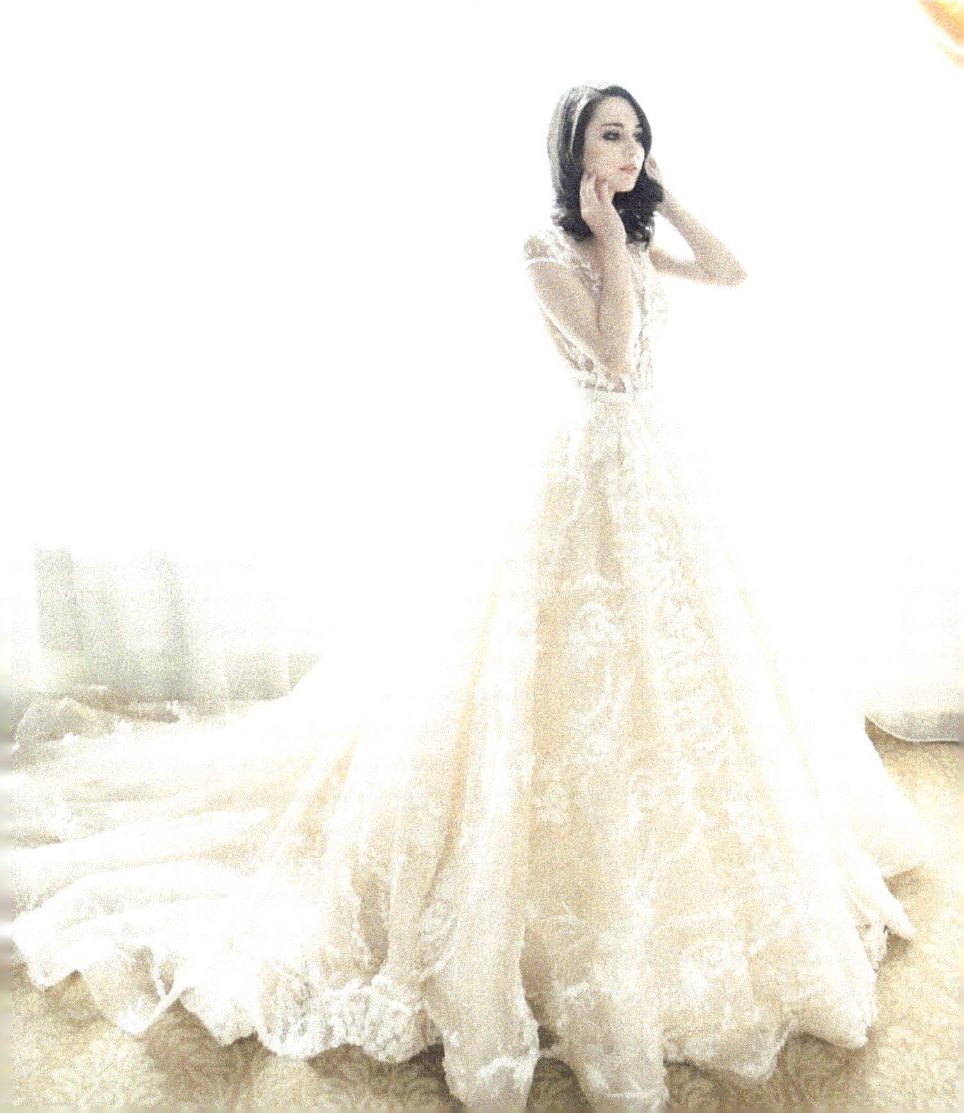

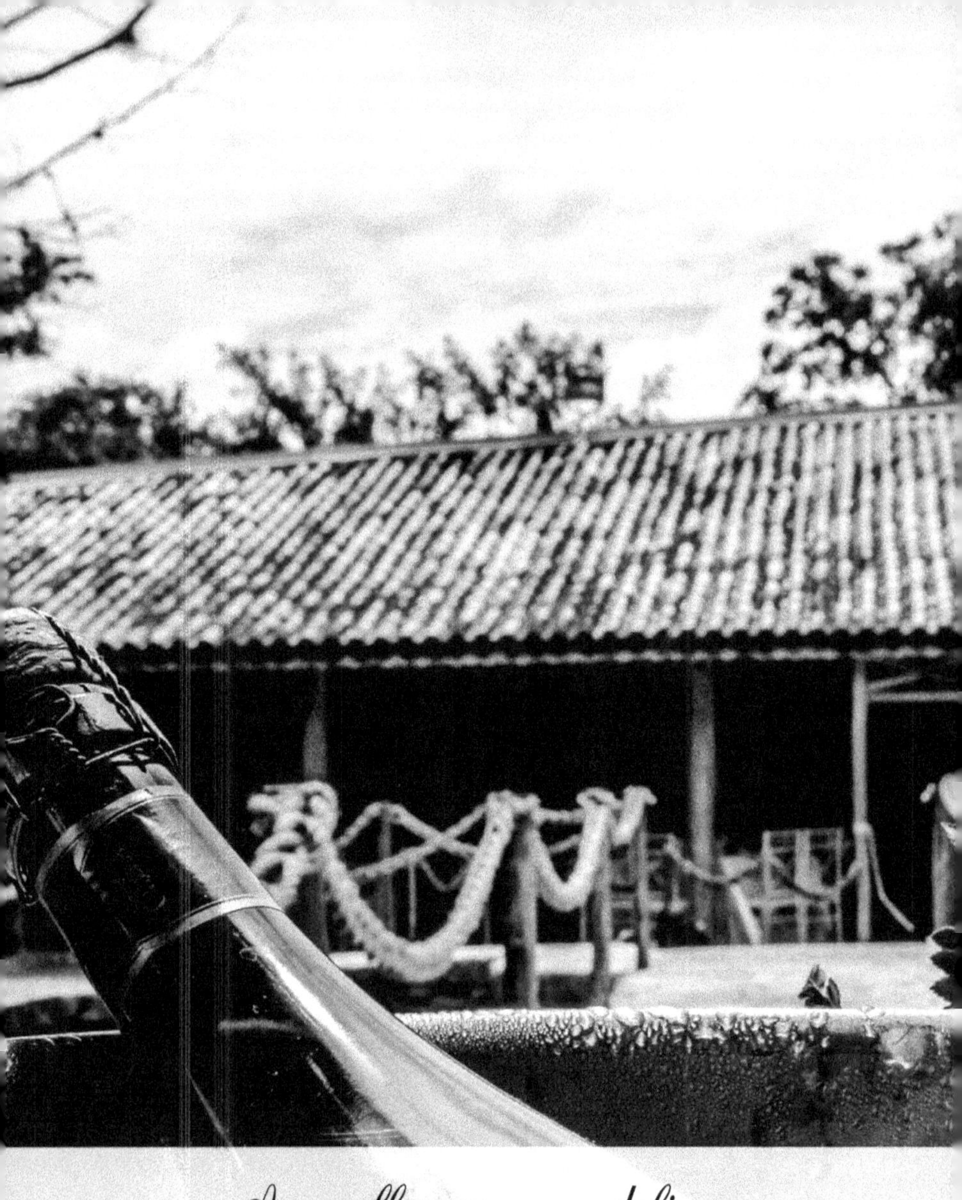

A small ceremony delivers
generous joy.

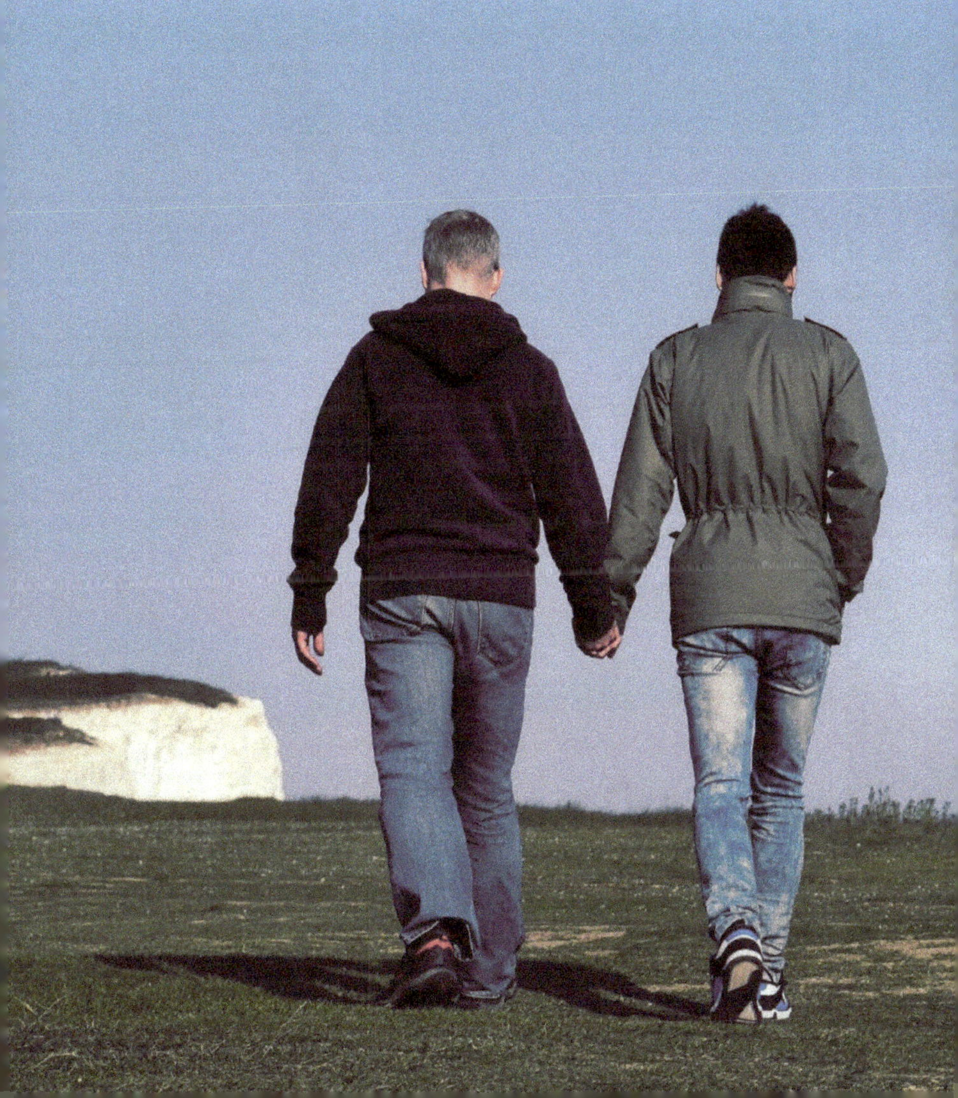

*The days before an event*

*focus the mind and soul.*

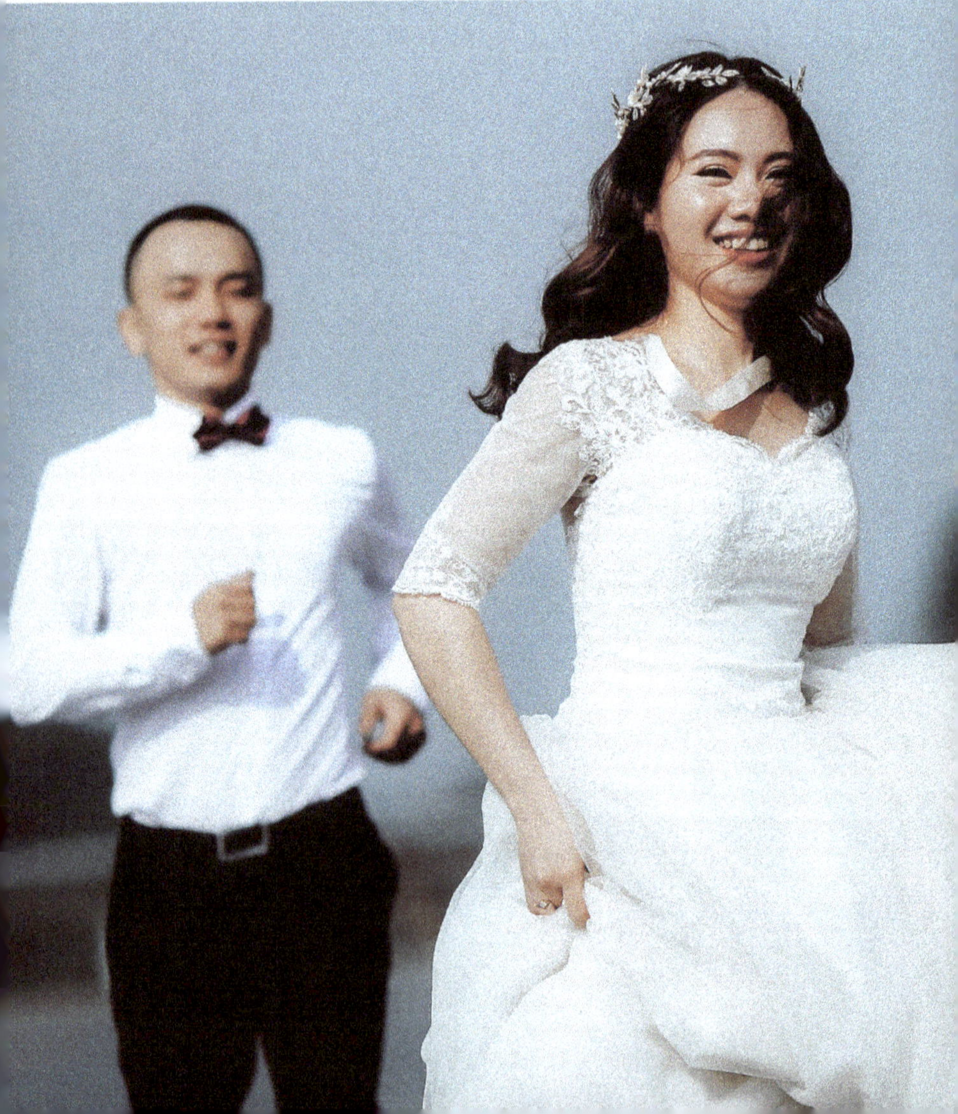

All can be forgiven
for the sake of celebration.

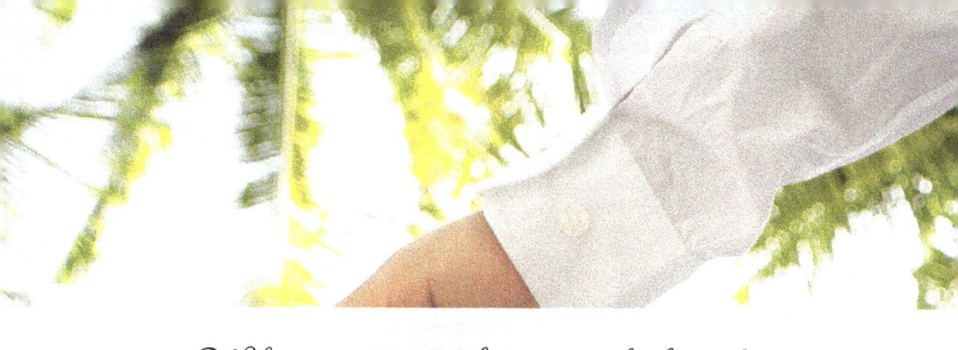

*When you feel overwhelmed,*
*friends provide shelter.*

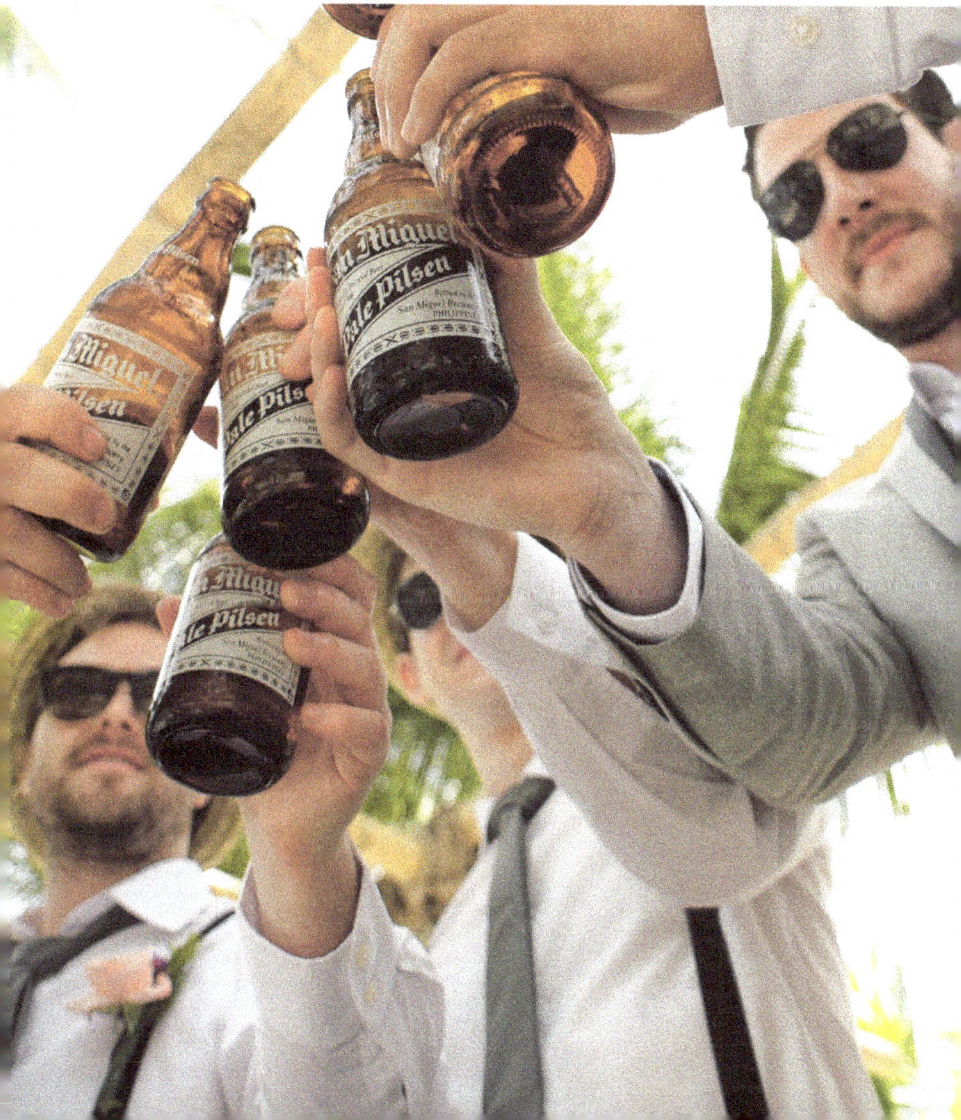

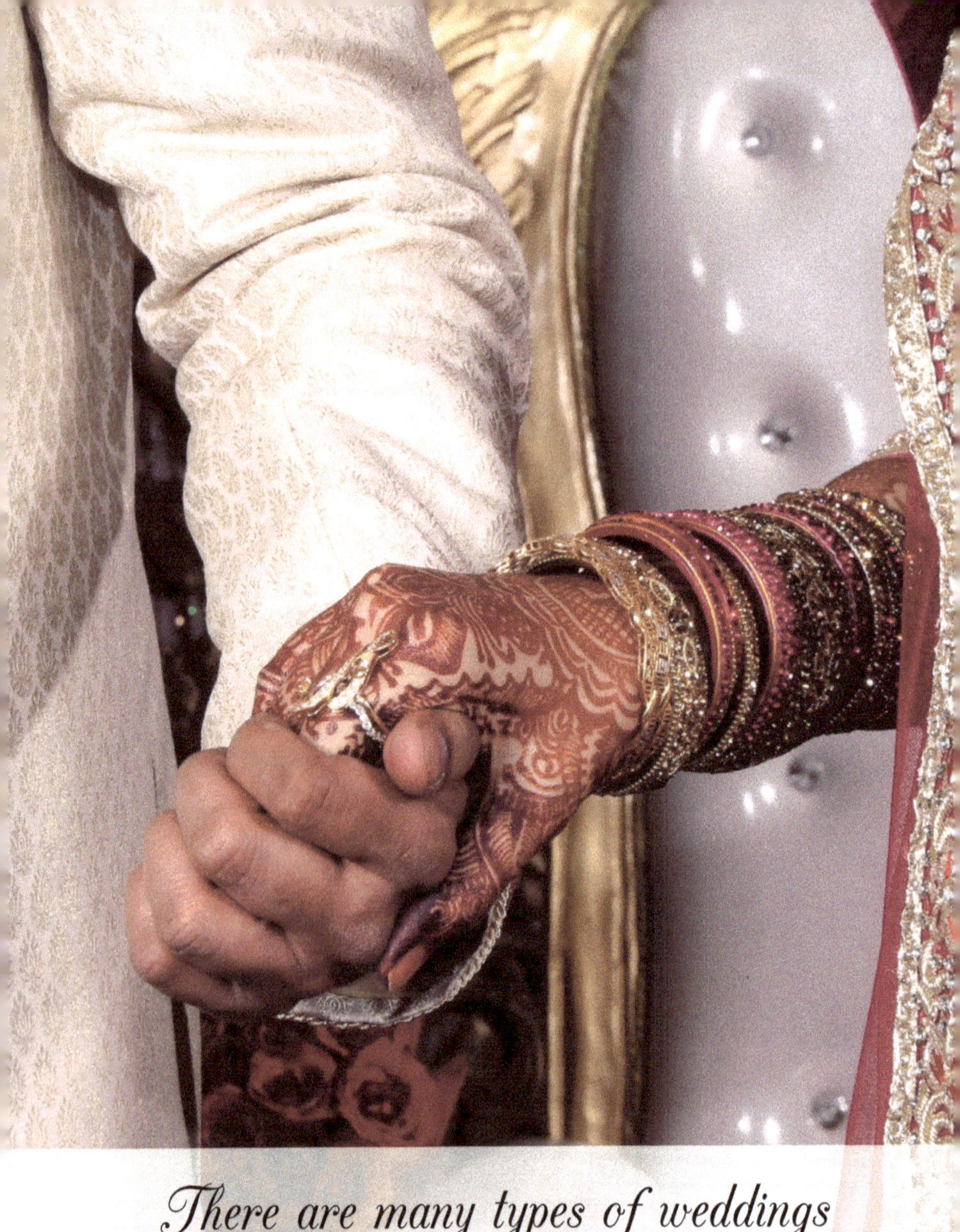

*There are many types of weddings
but only one commitment.*

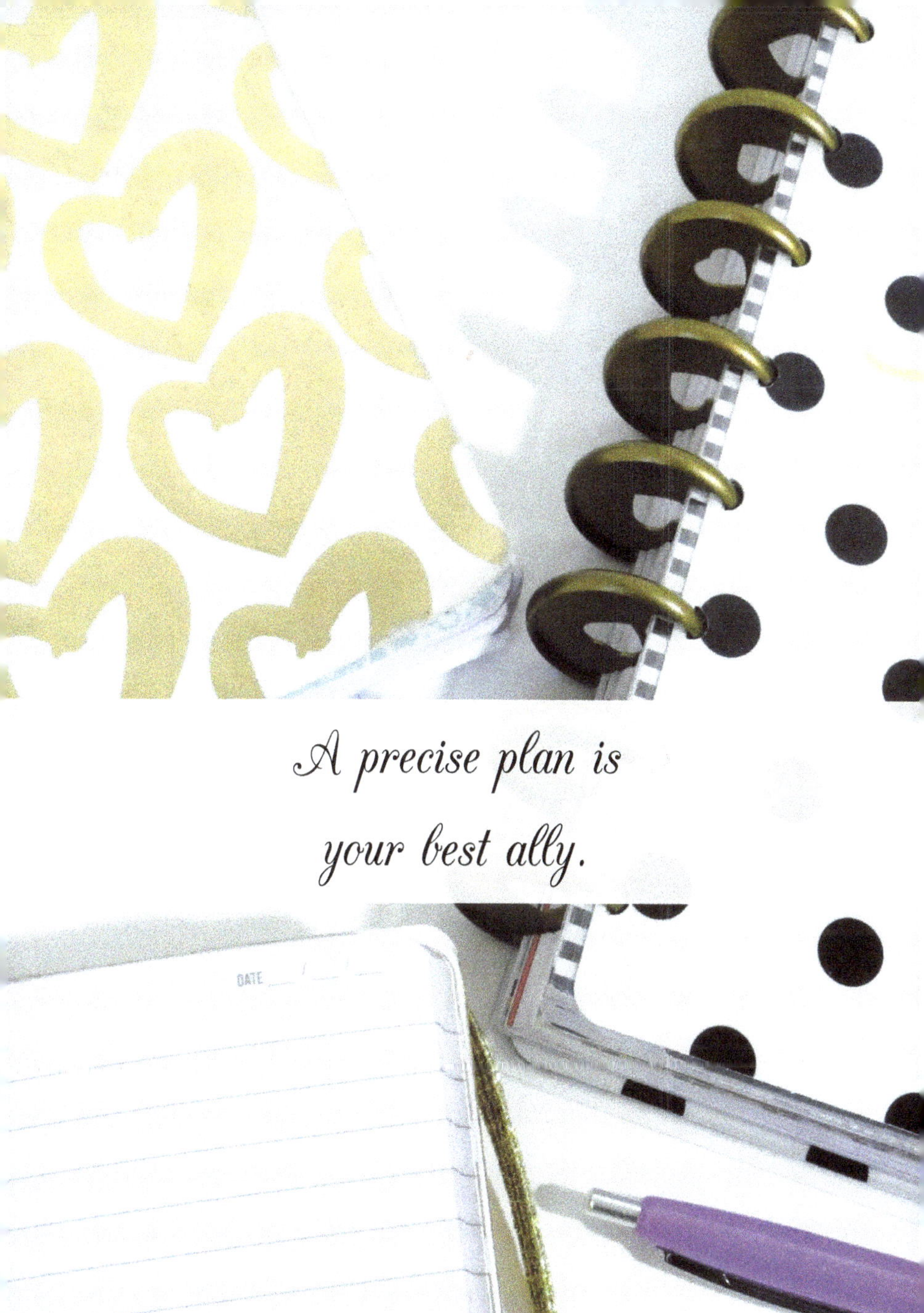

A precise plan is
your best ally.

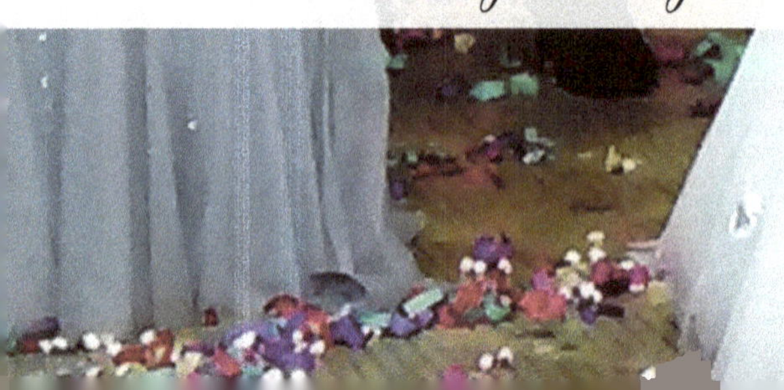

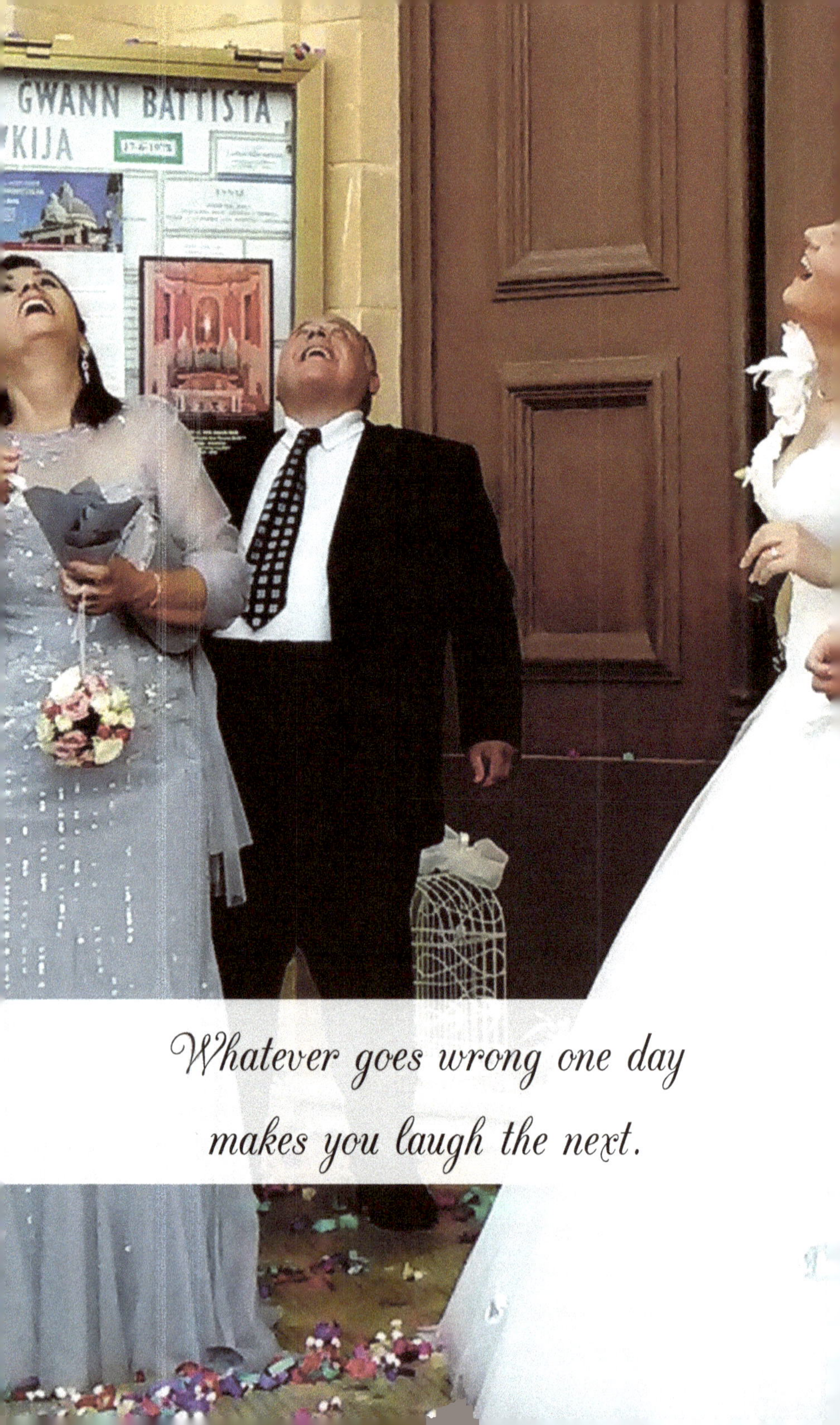

Whatever goes wrong one day
makes you laugh the next.

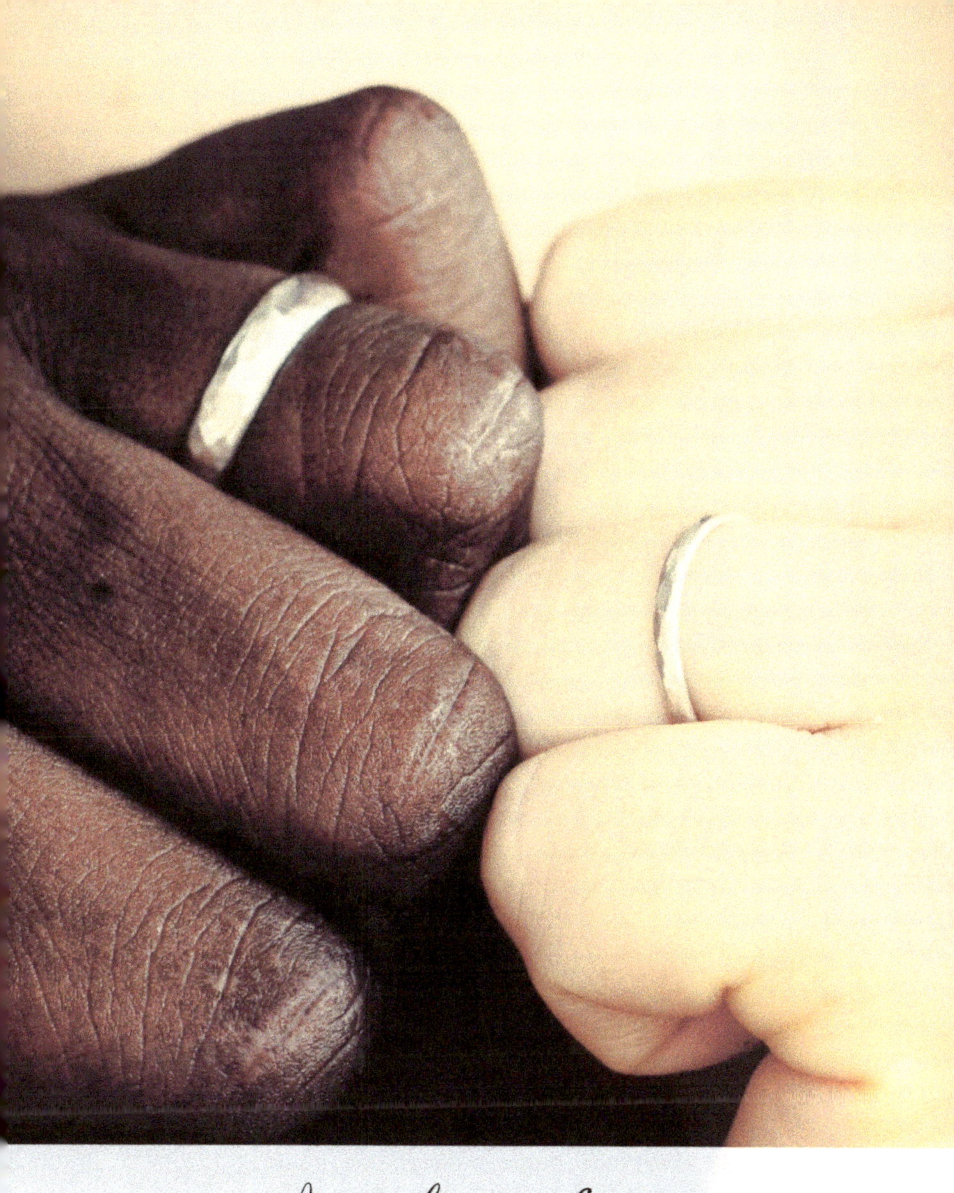

A simple ring forms
a profound symbol.

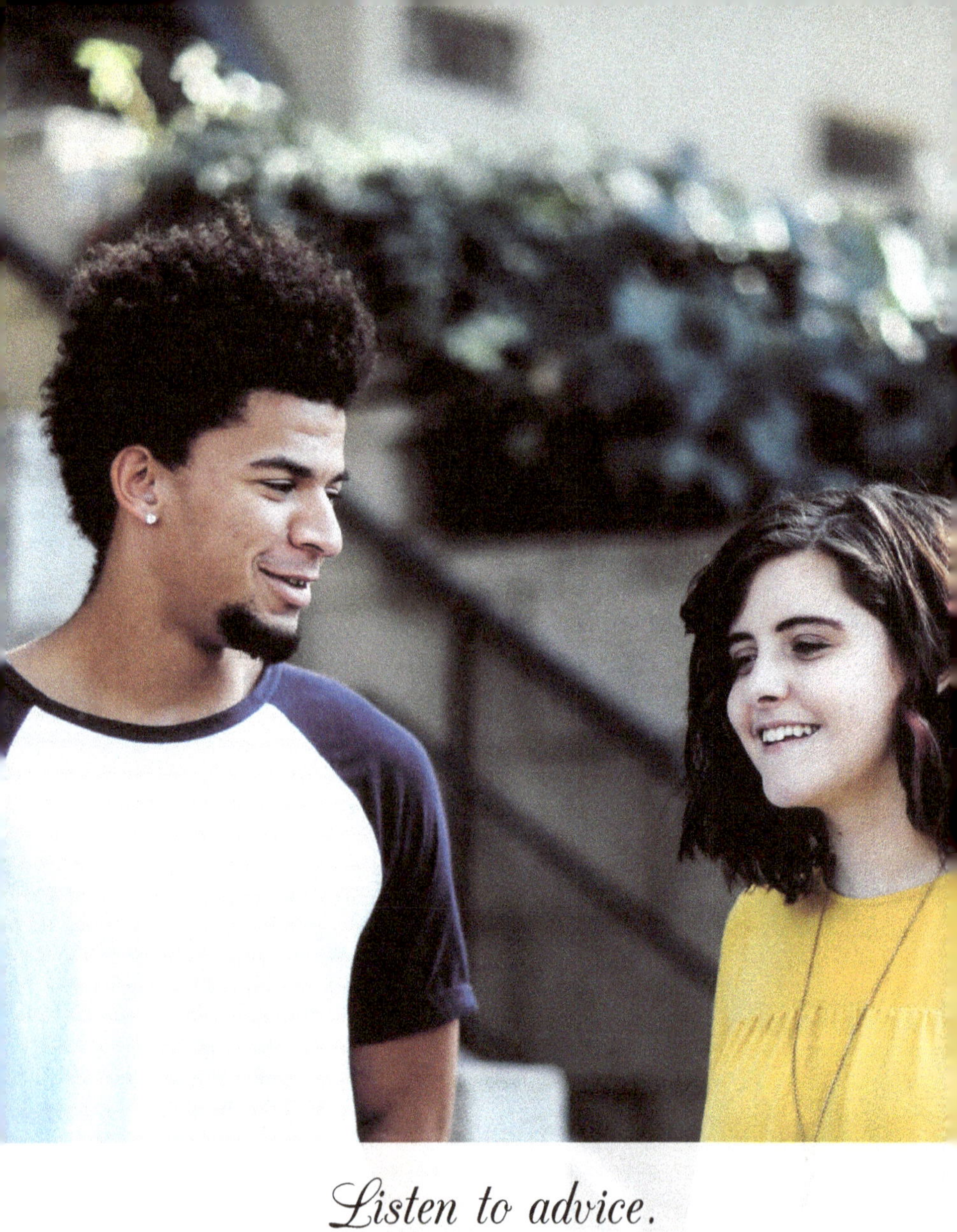

Listen to advice.

Then decide for yourself.

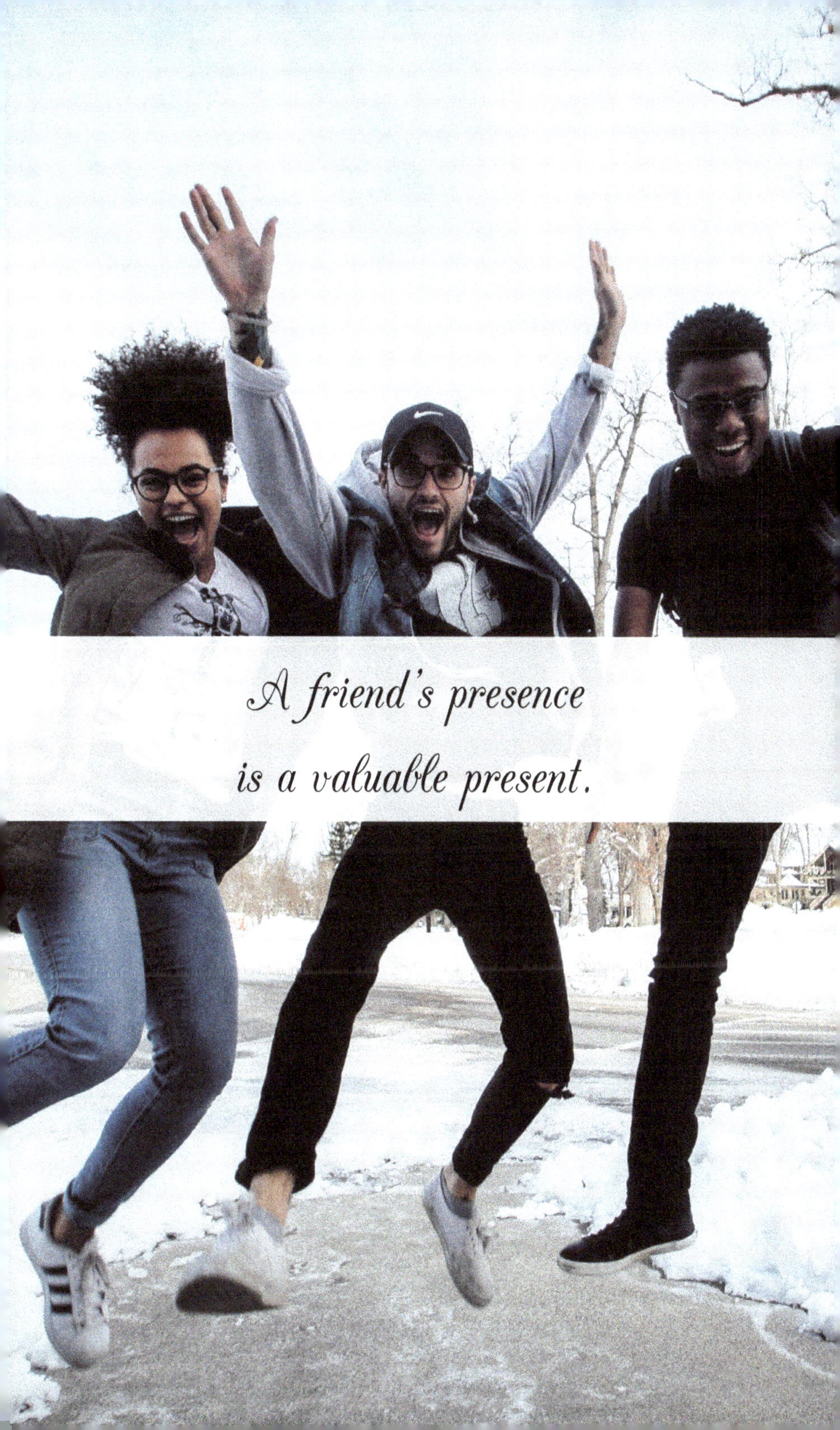

A friend's presence

is a valuable present.

*Vows made with love are vows that build love.*

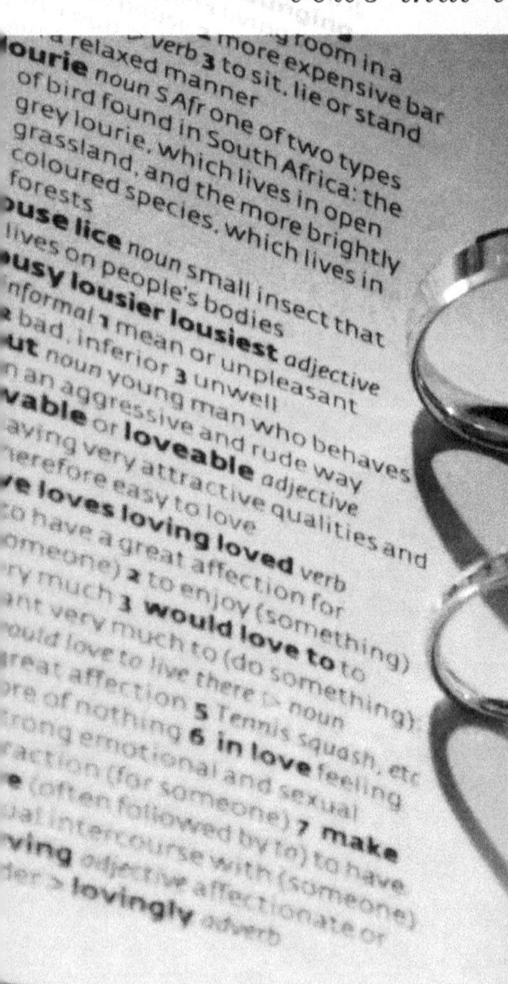

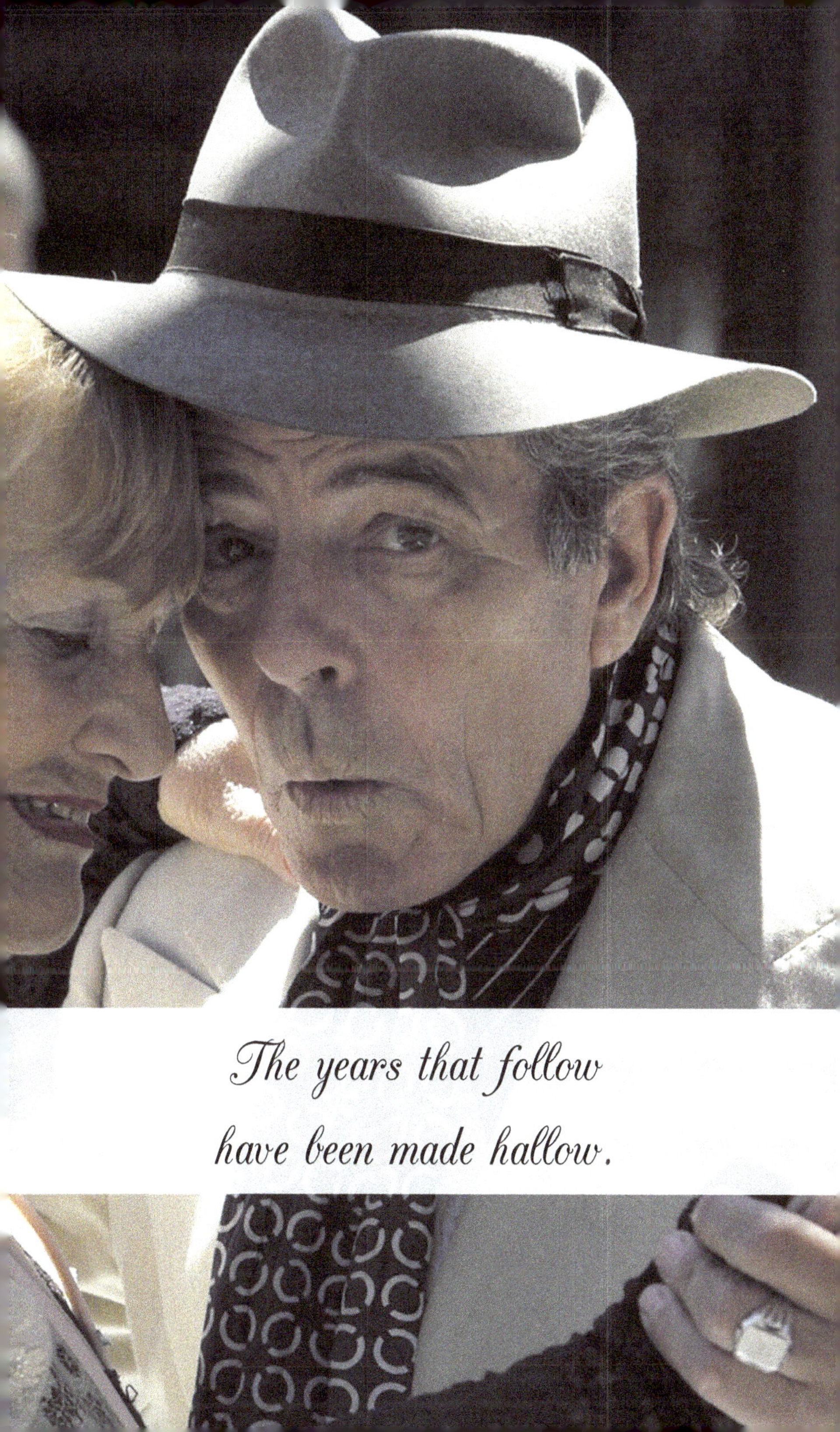

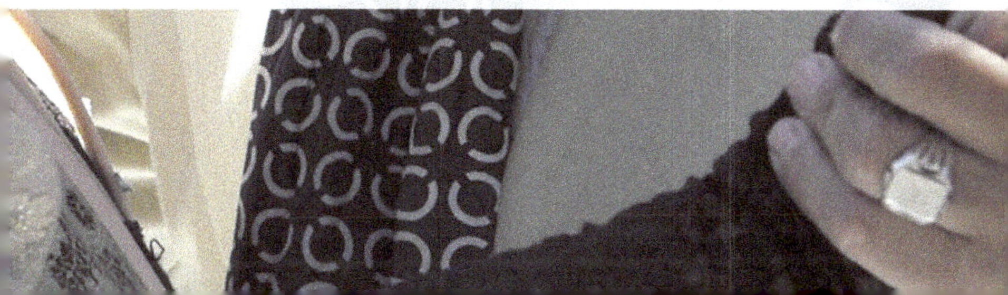

The years that follow
have been made hallow.

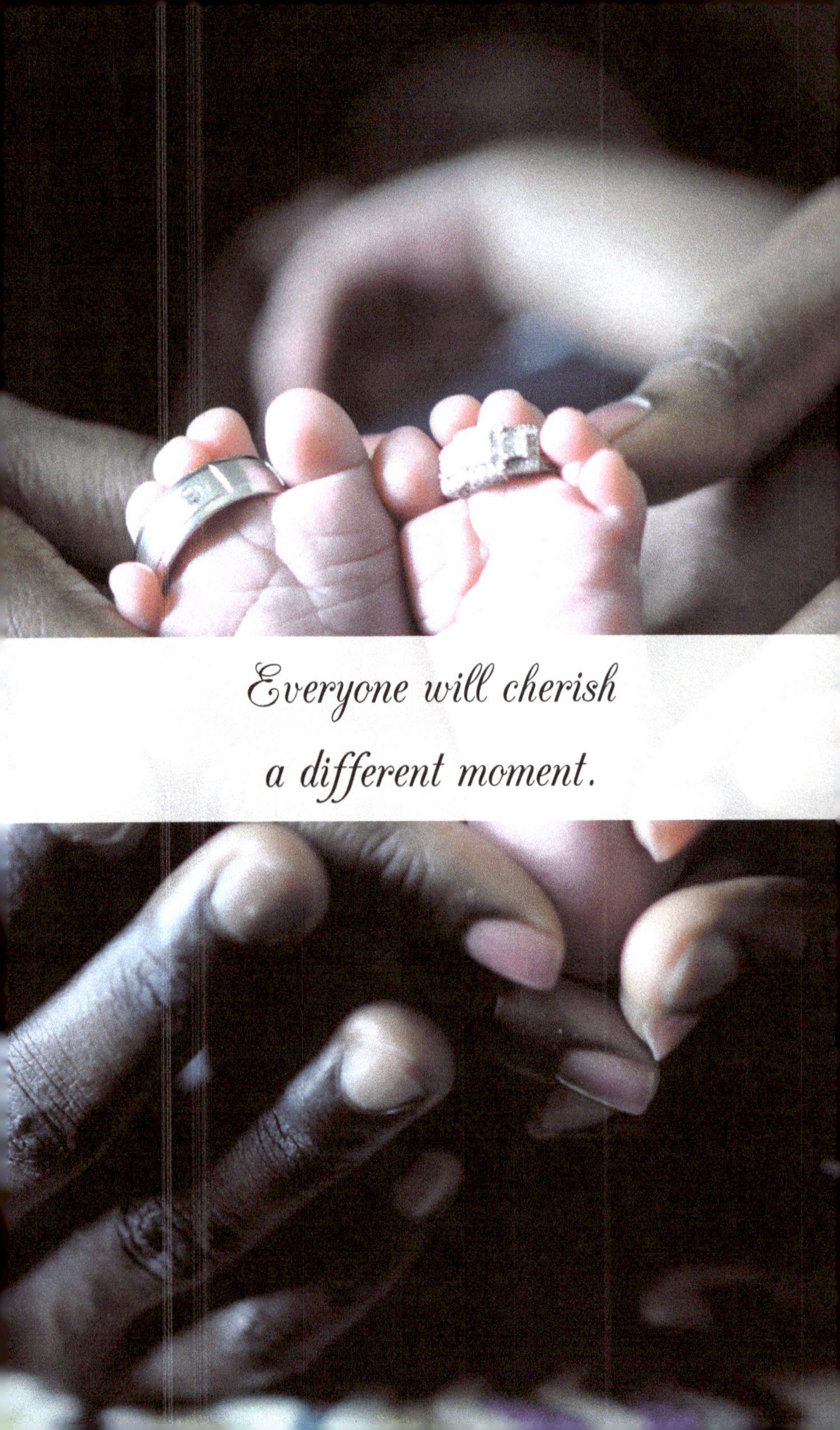

Everyone will cherish

a different moment.

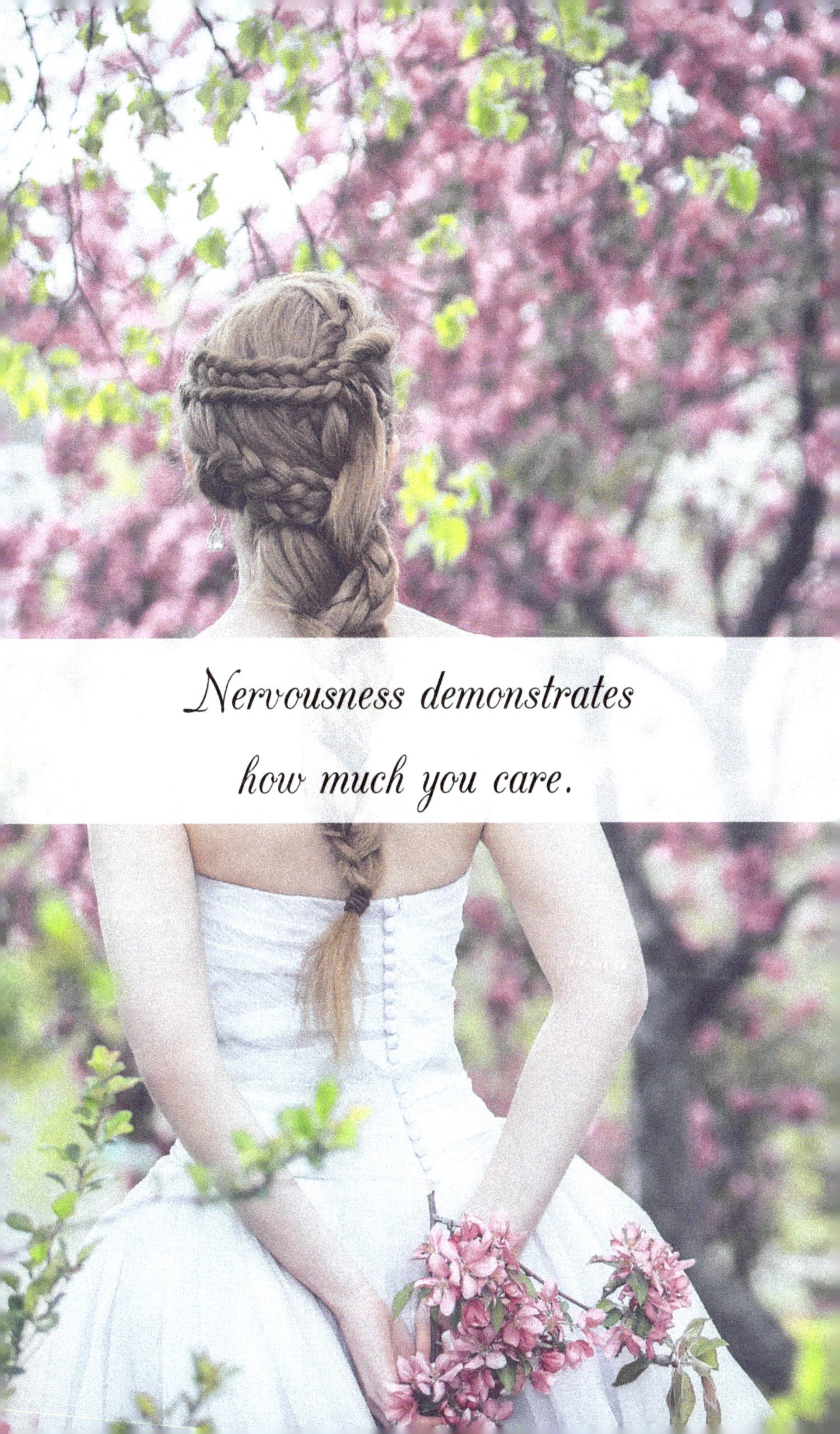

Nervousness demonstrates
how much you care.

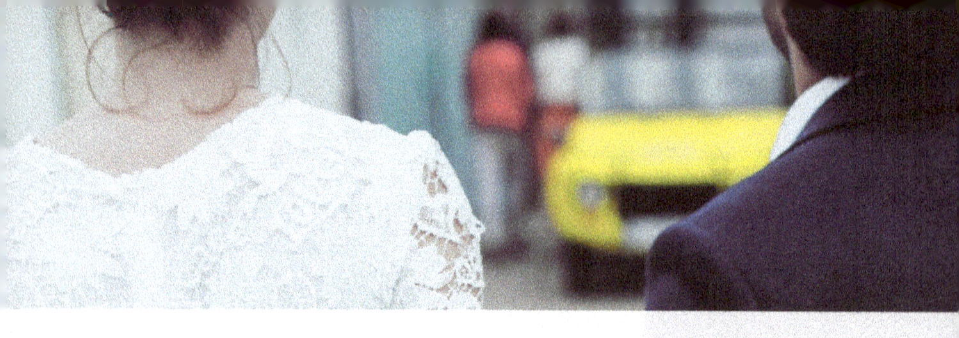

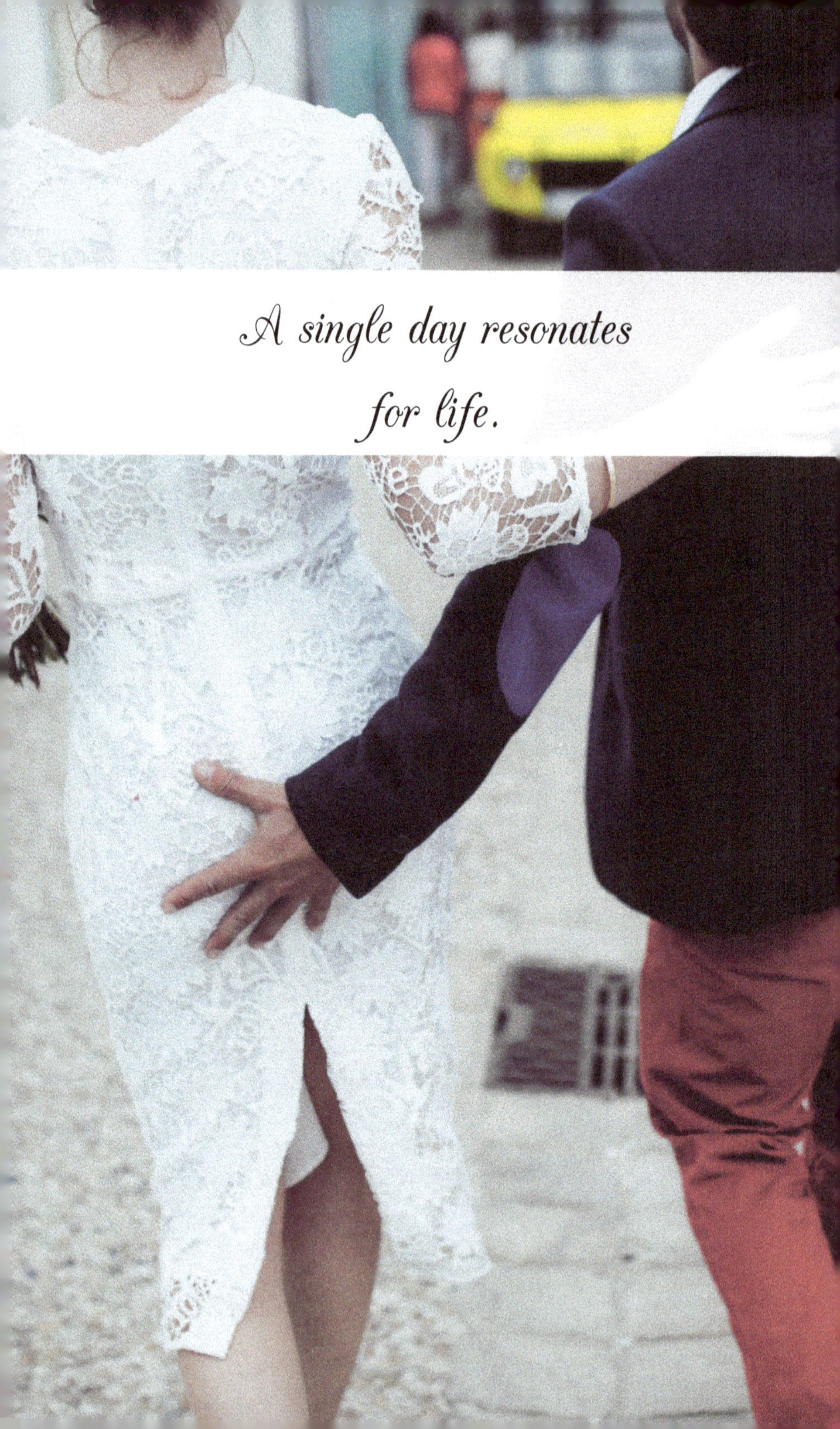

A single day resonates
for life.

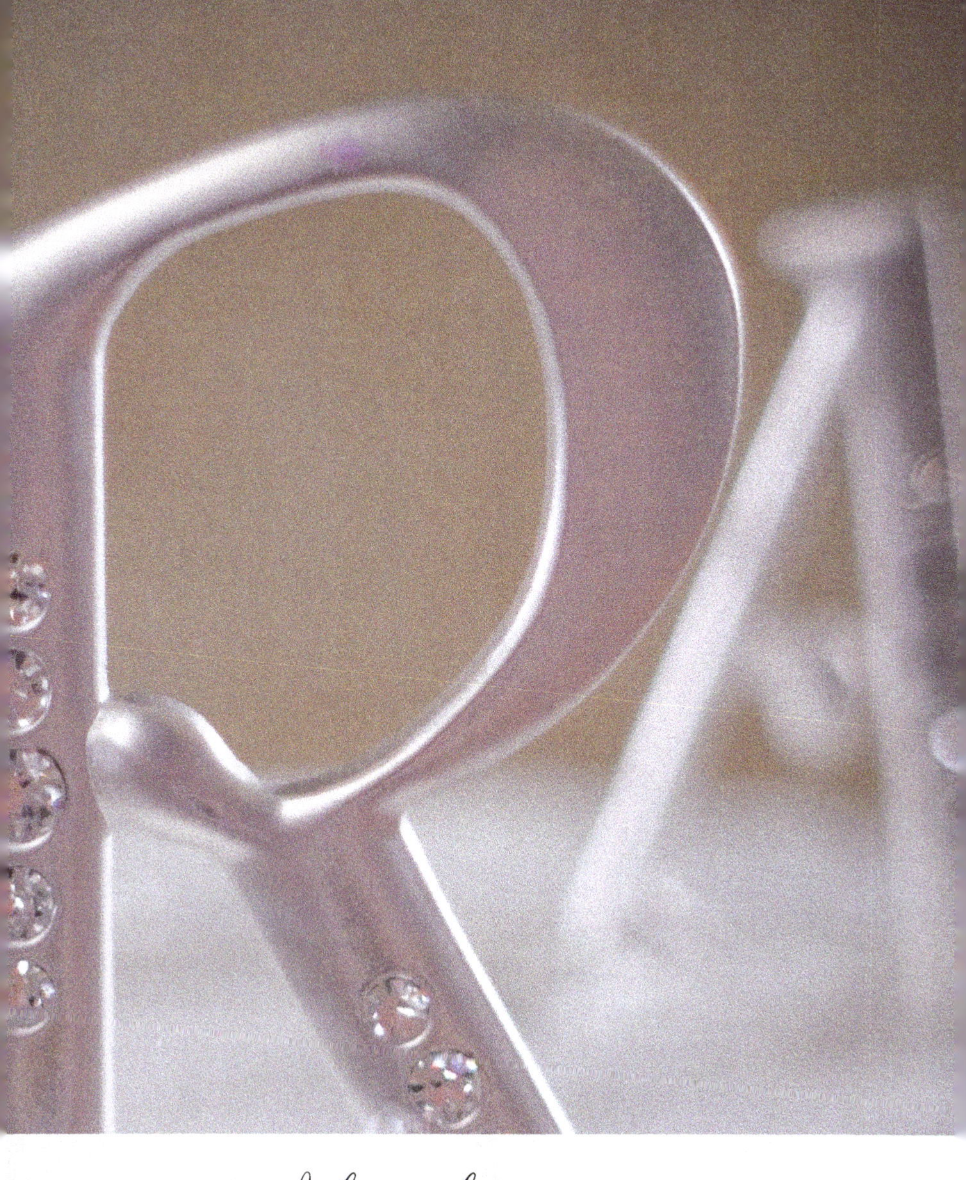

A keepsake preserves
bounteous memories.

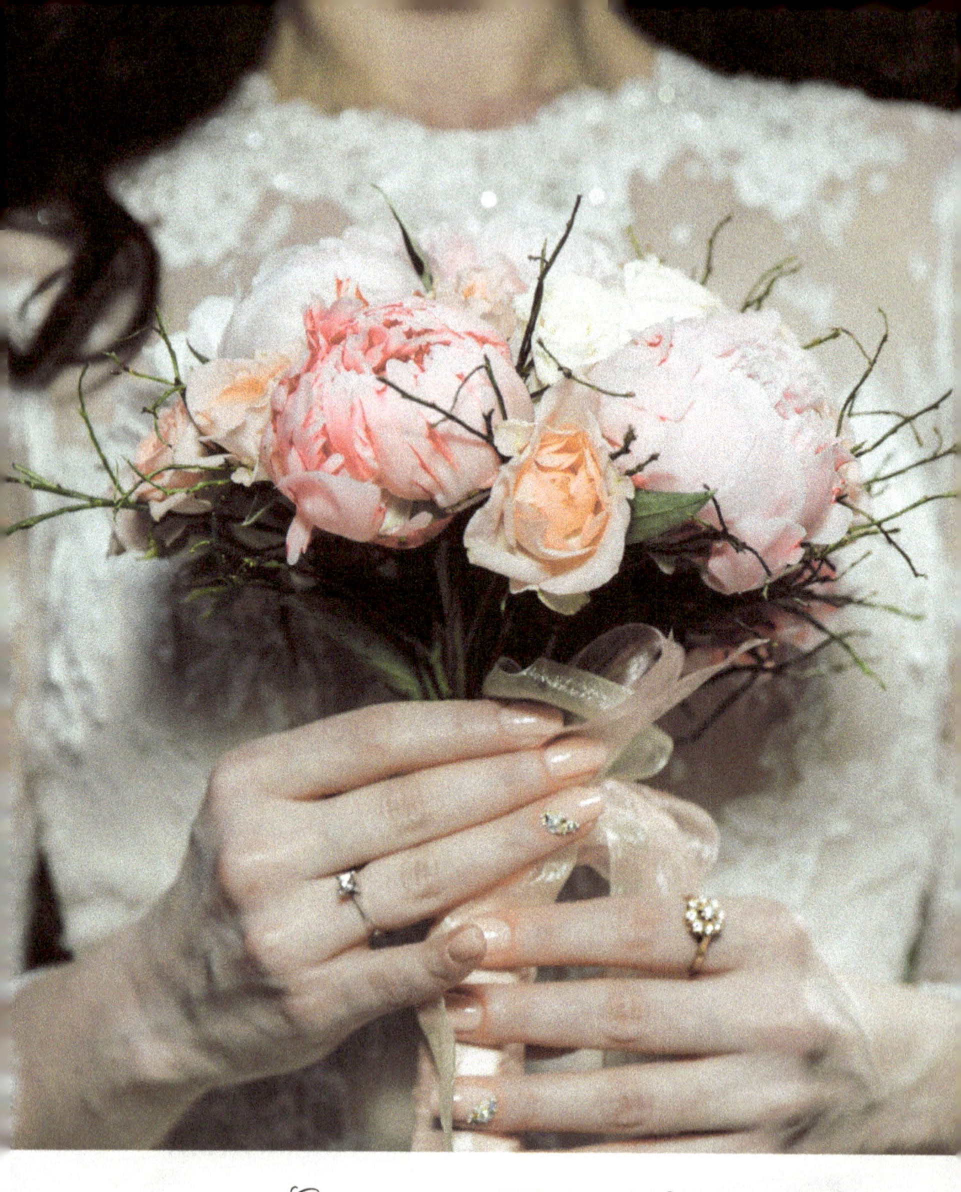

Every step forward is
also a step toward.

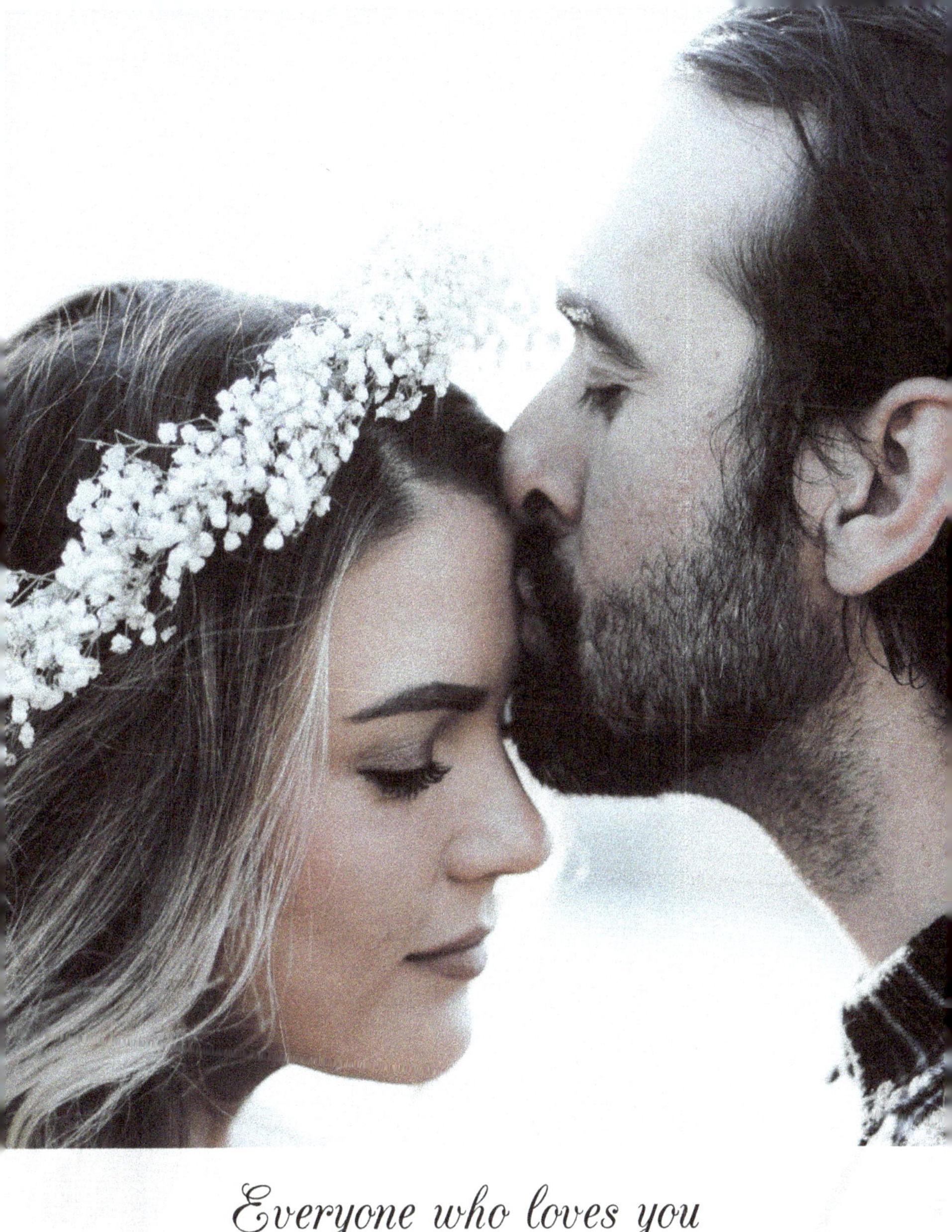

Everyone who loves you
wants the best for you.

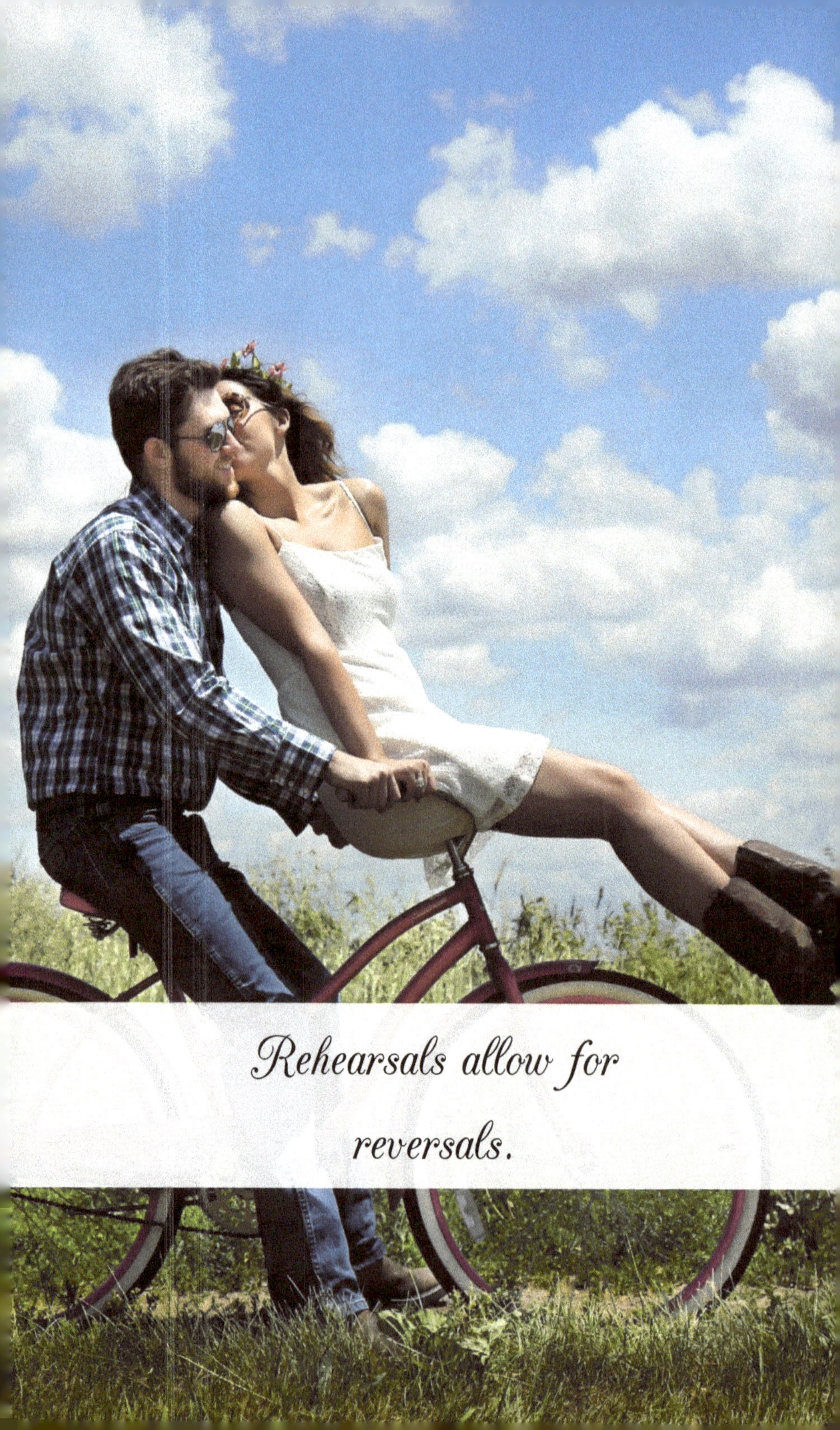

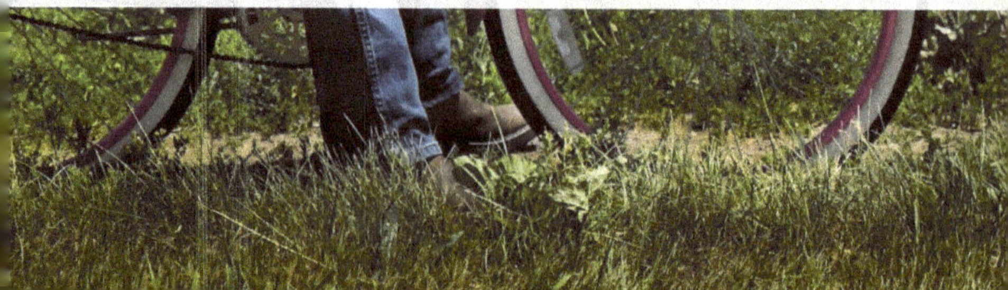

Rehearsals allow for reversals.

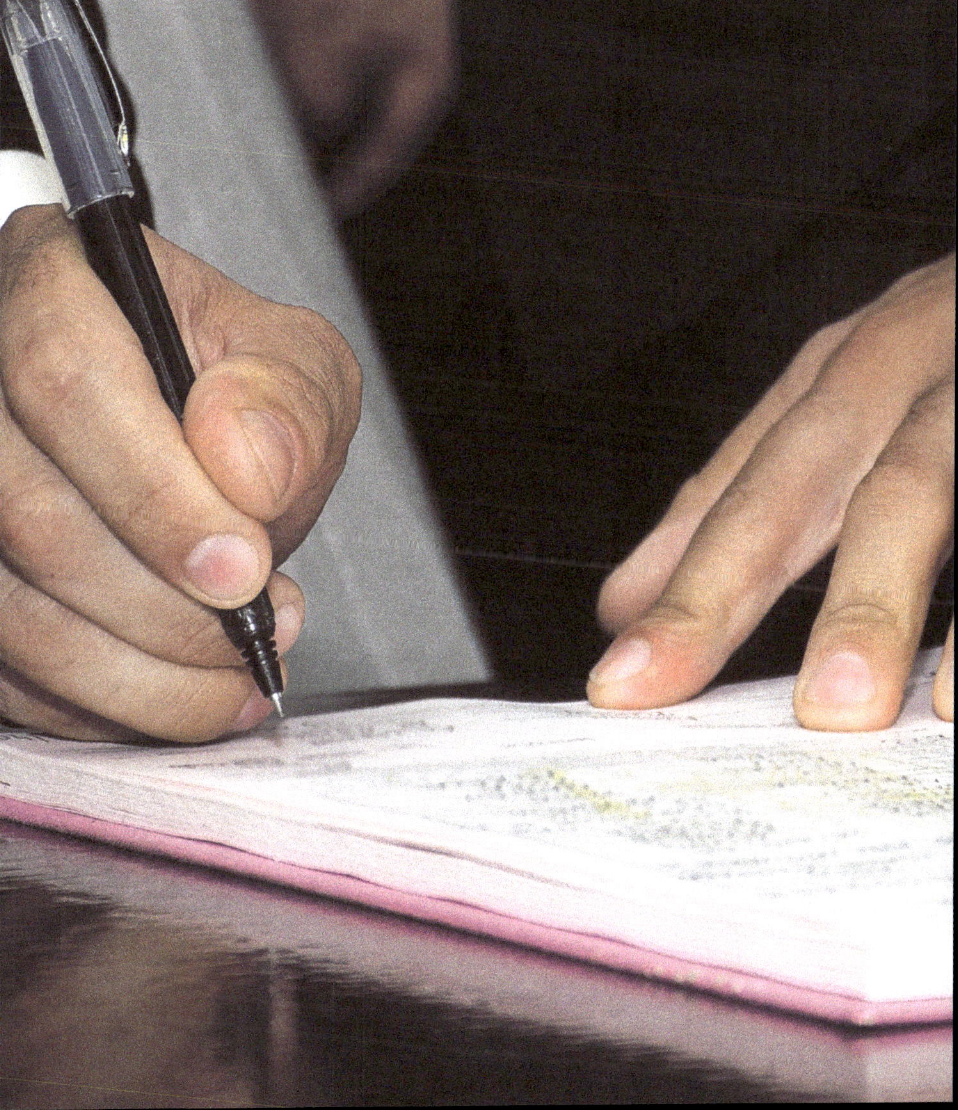
A guest list is a
map of relationships.

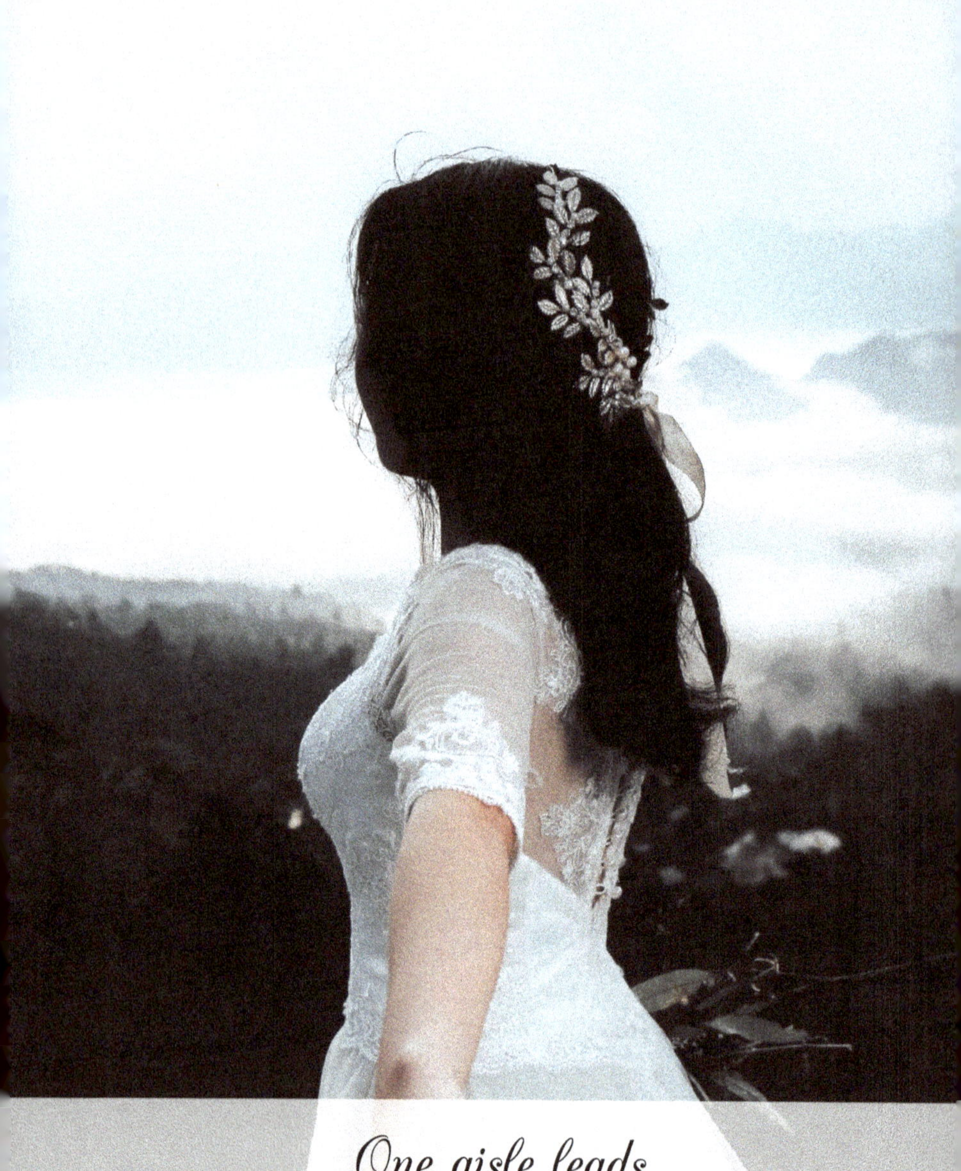

One aisle leads
to many roads.

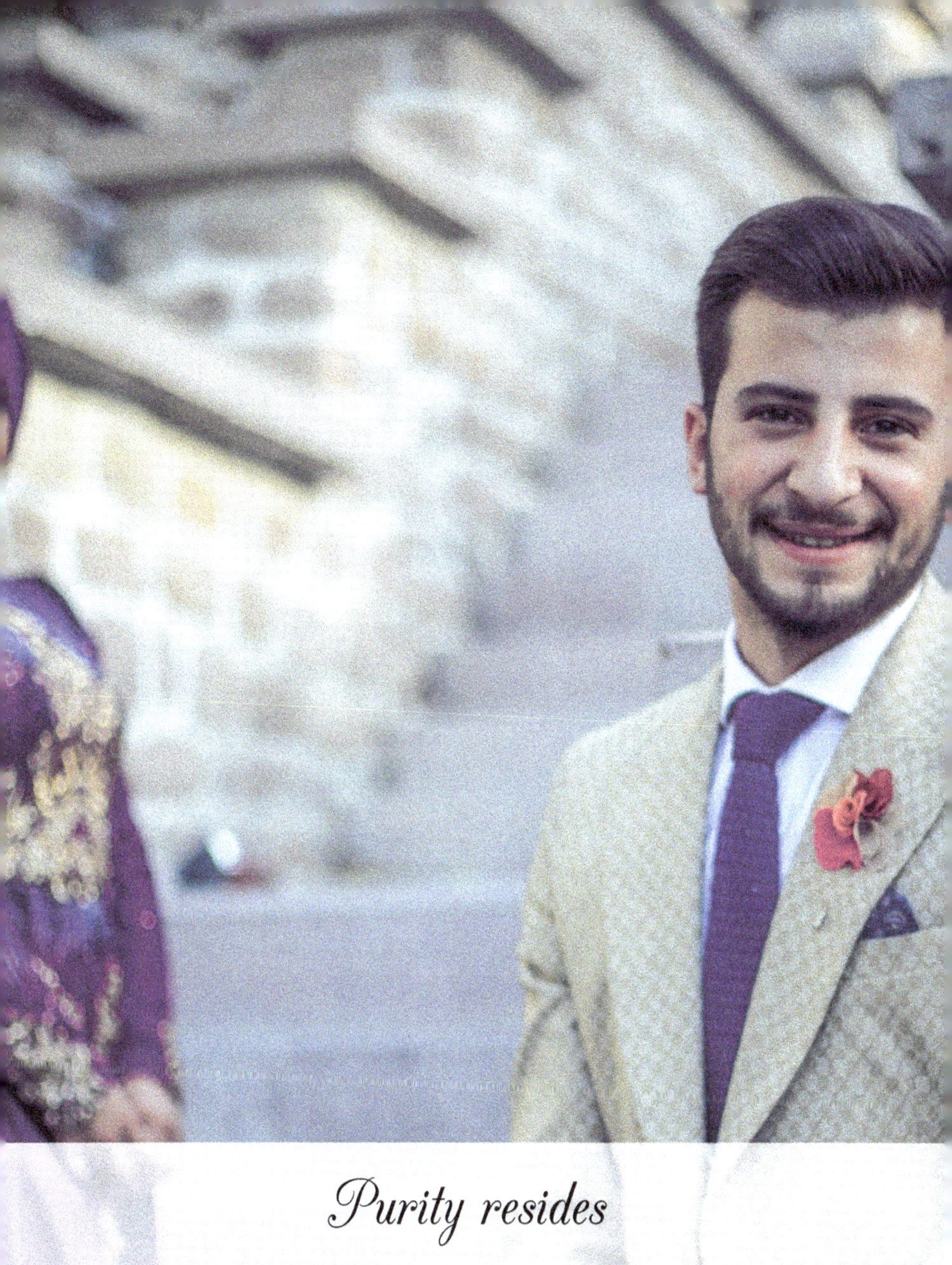


Purity resides
in the loving heart.

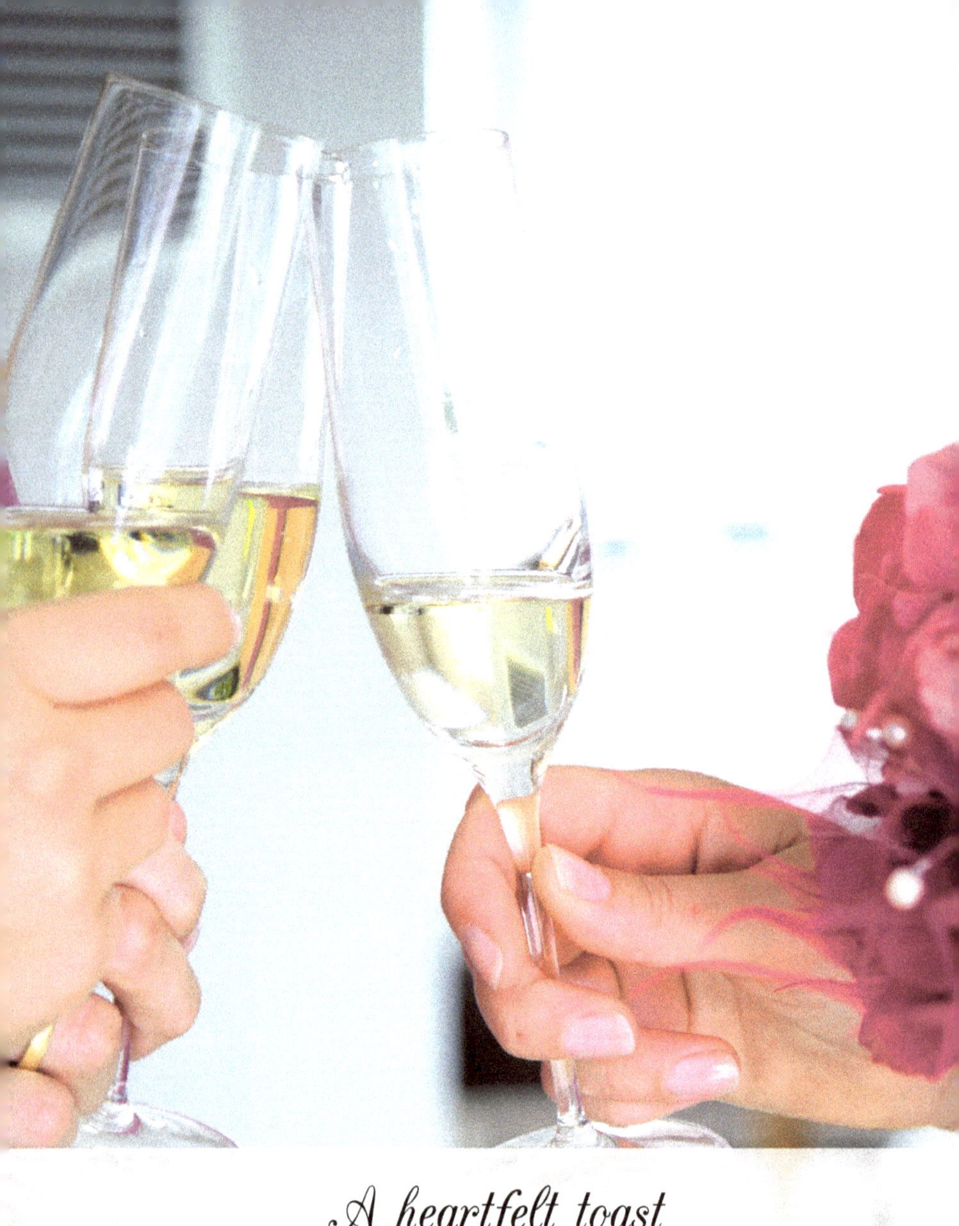


A heartfelt toast

rings across the years.

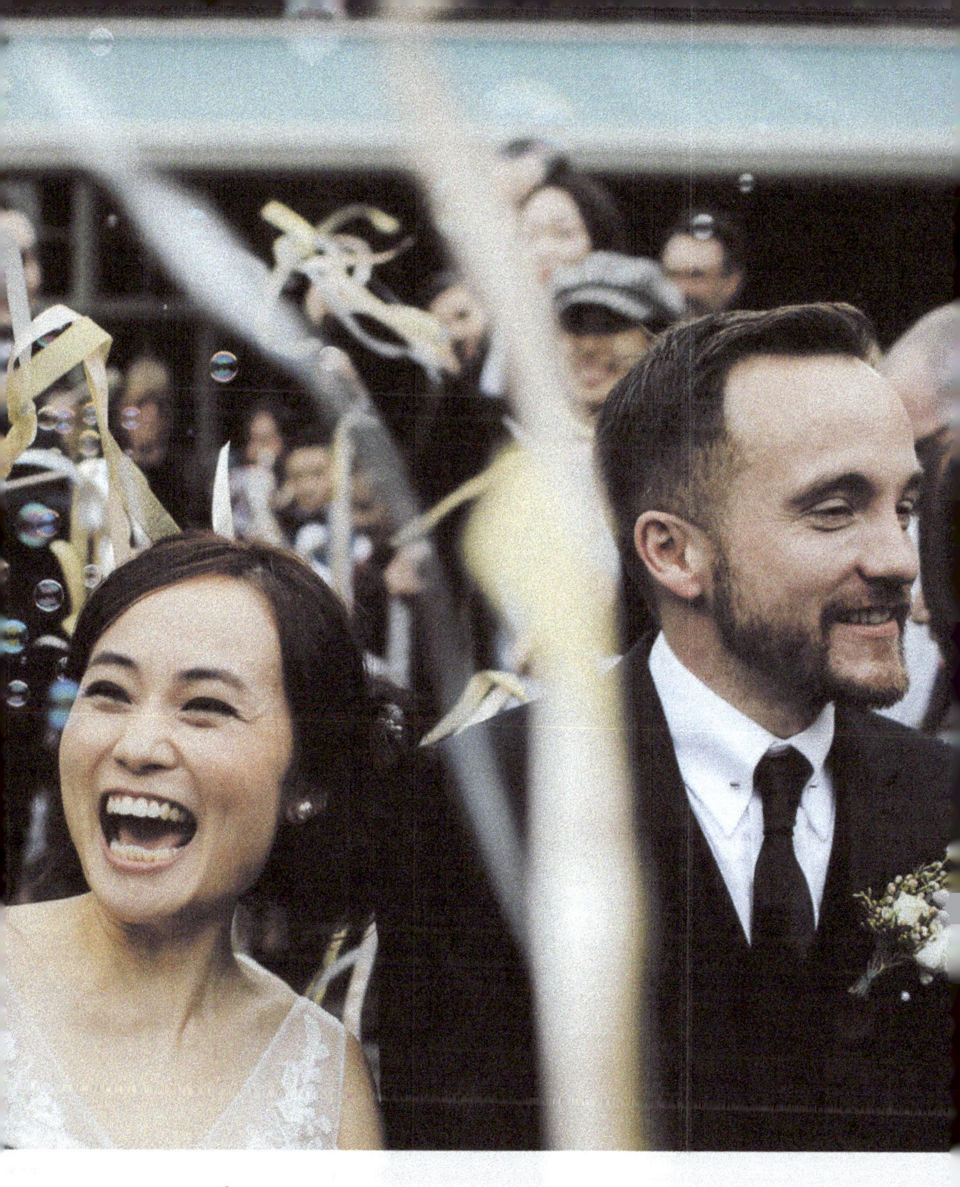
Some things might go wrong.
Many things will go right.

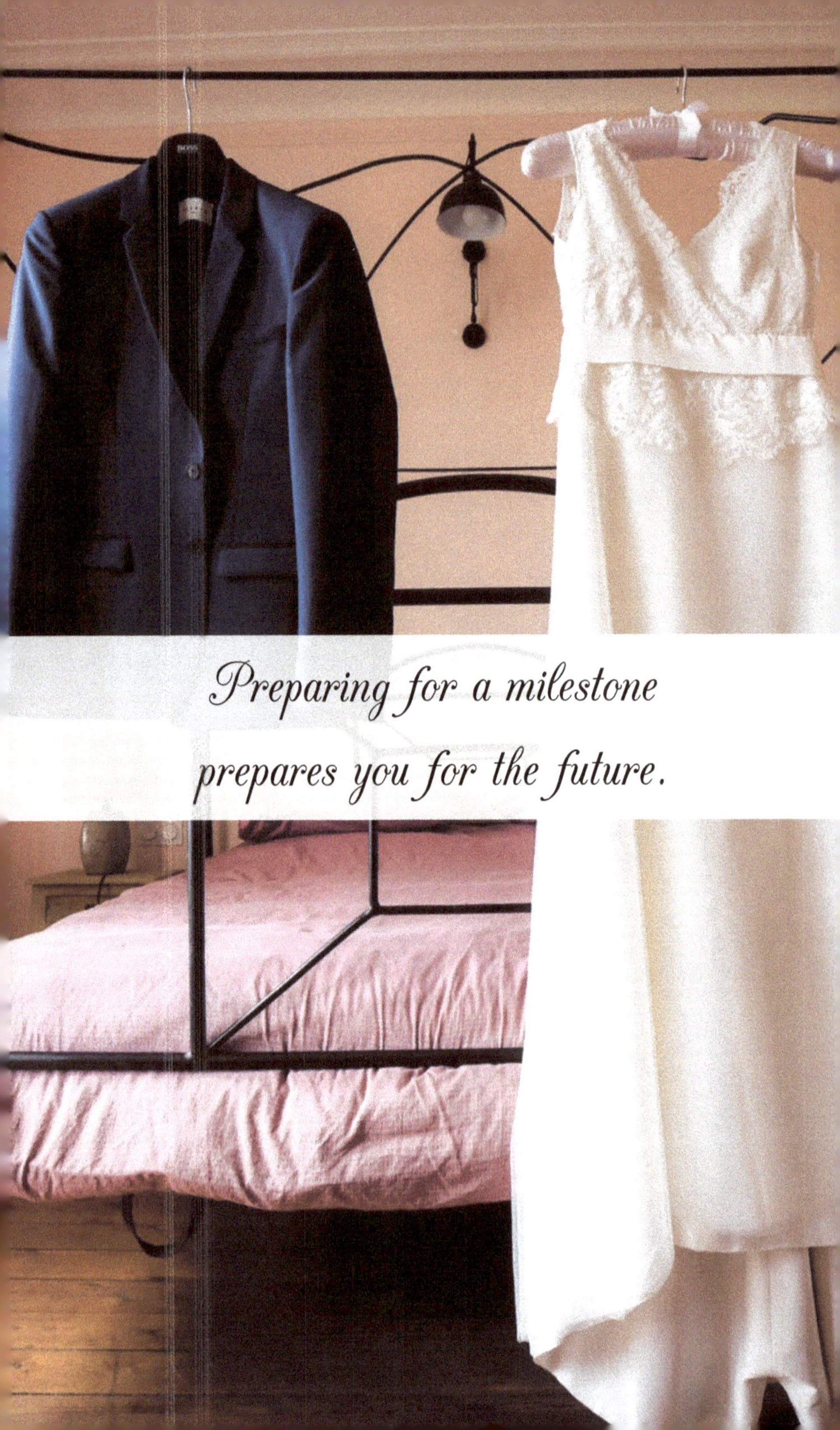

Preparing for a milestone

prepares you for the future.

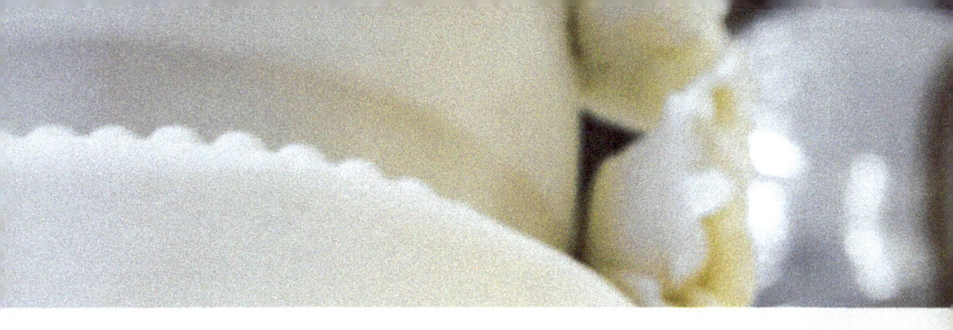

The sweetness of cake portends
the sweetness to come.

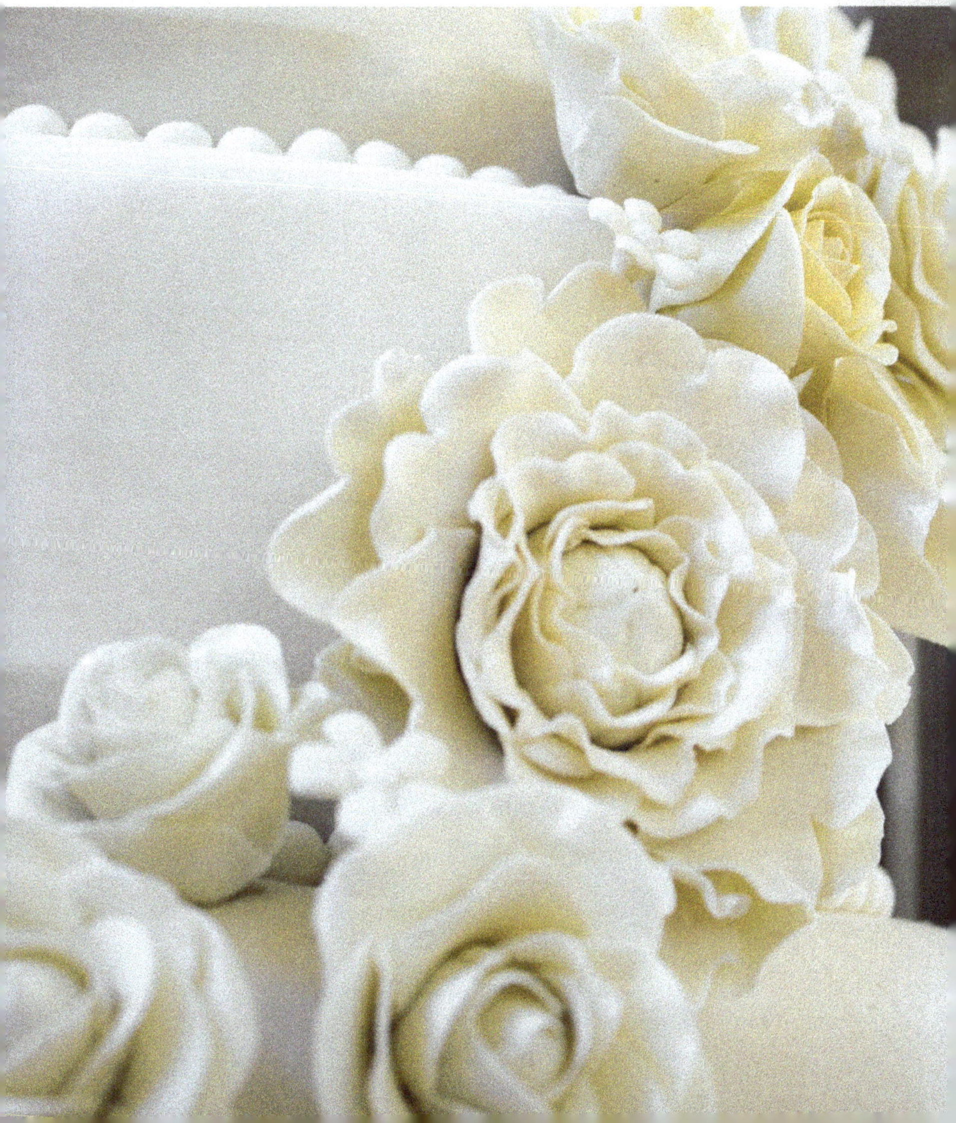

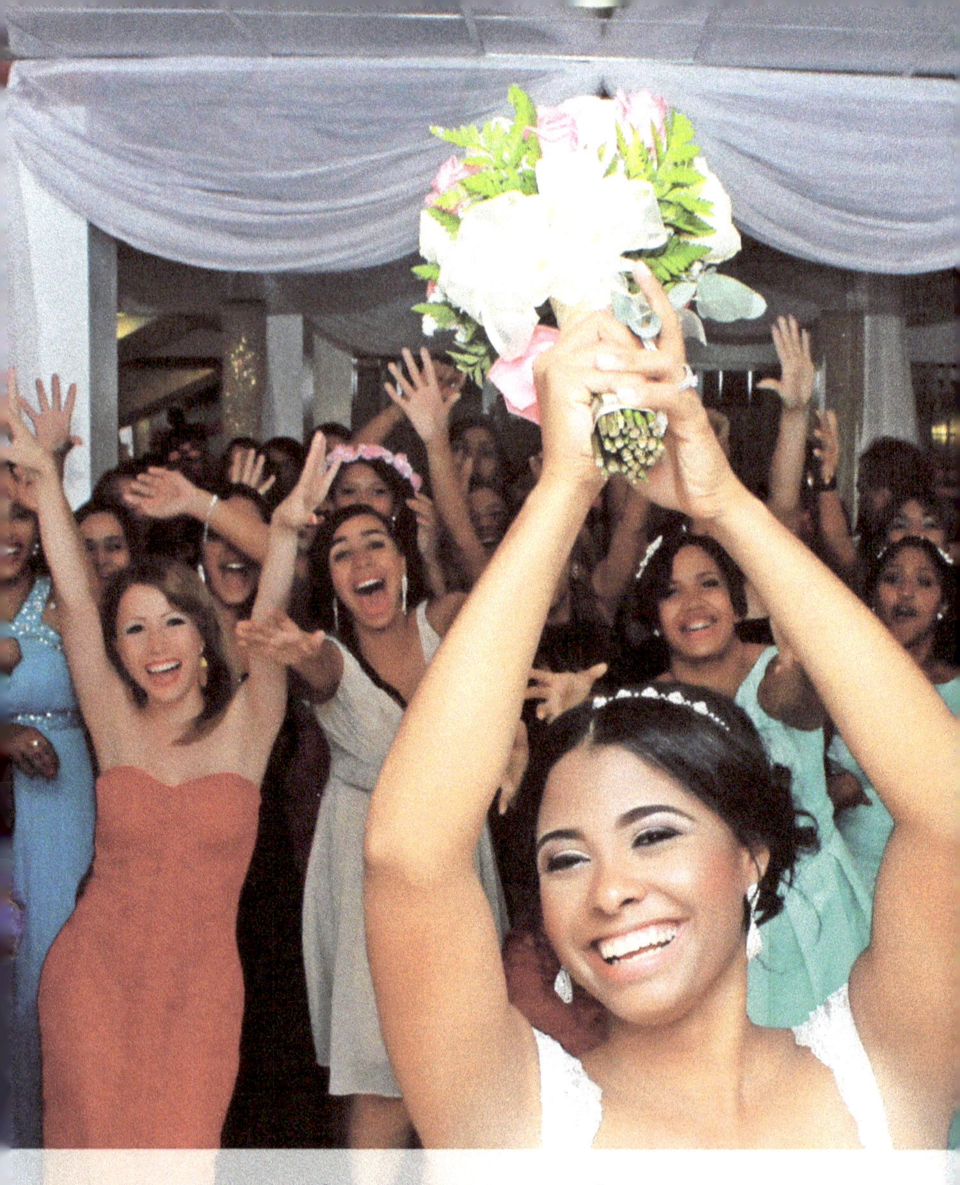

Bouquets are fleeting.
Memories endure.

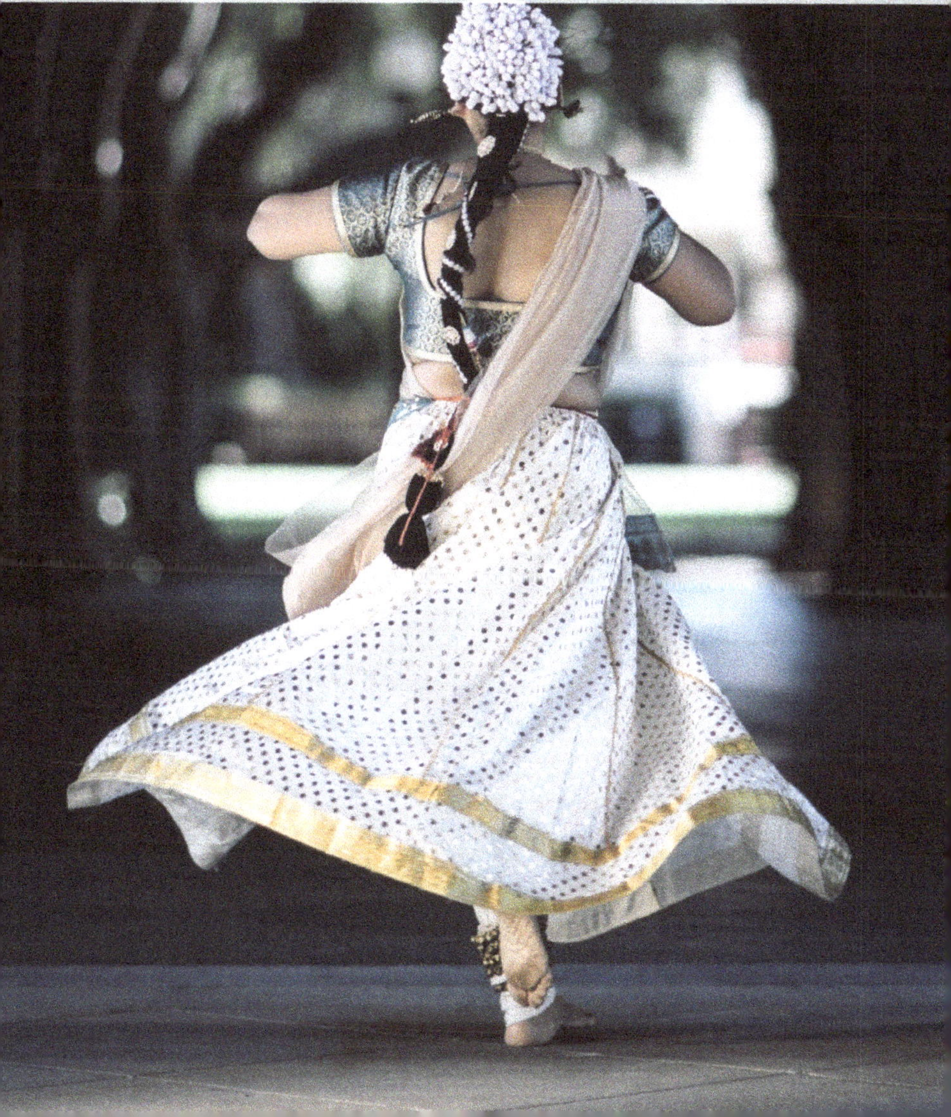
The heart guides the
long and wonderful journey.

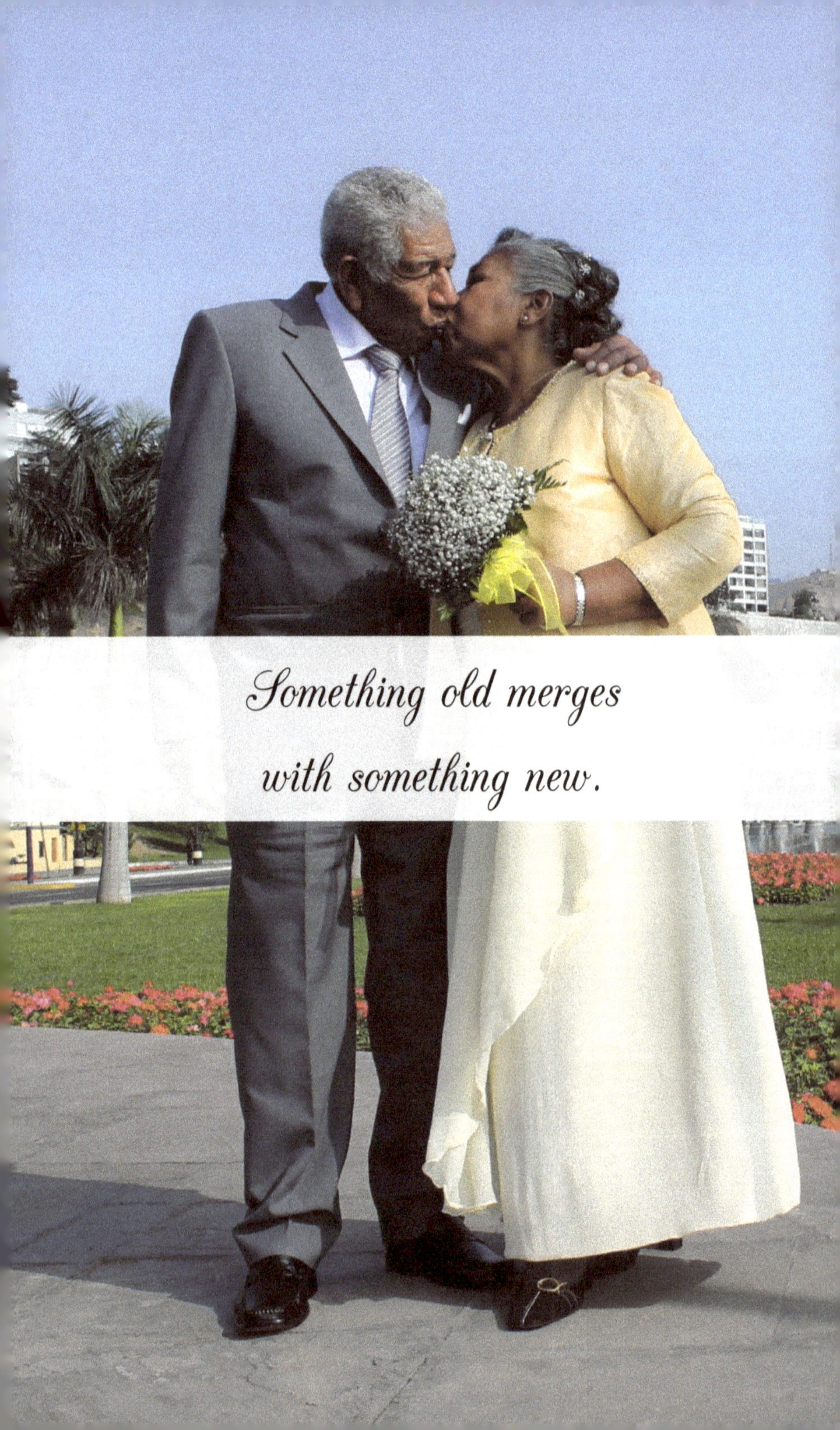

Something old merges
with something new.

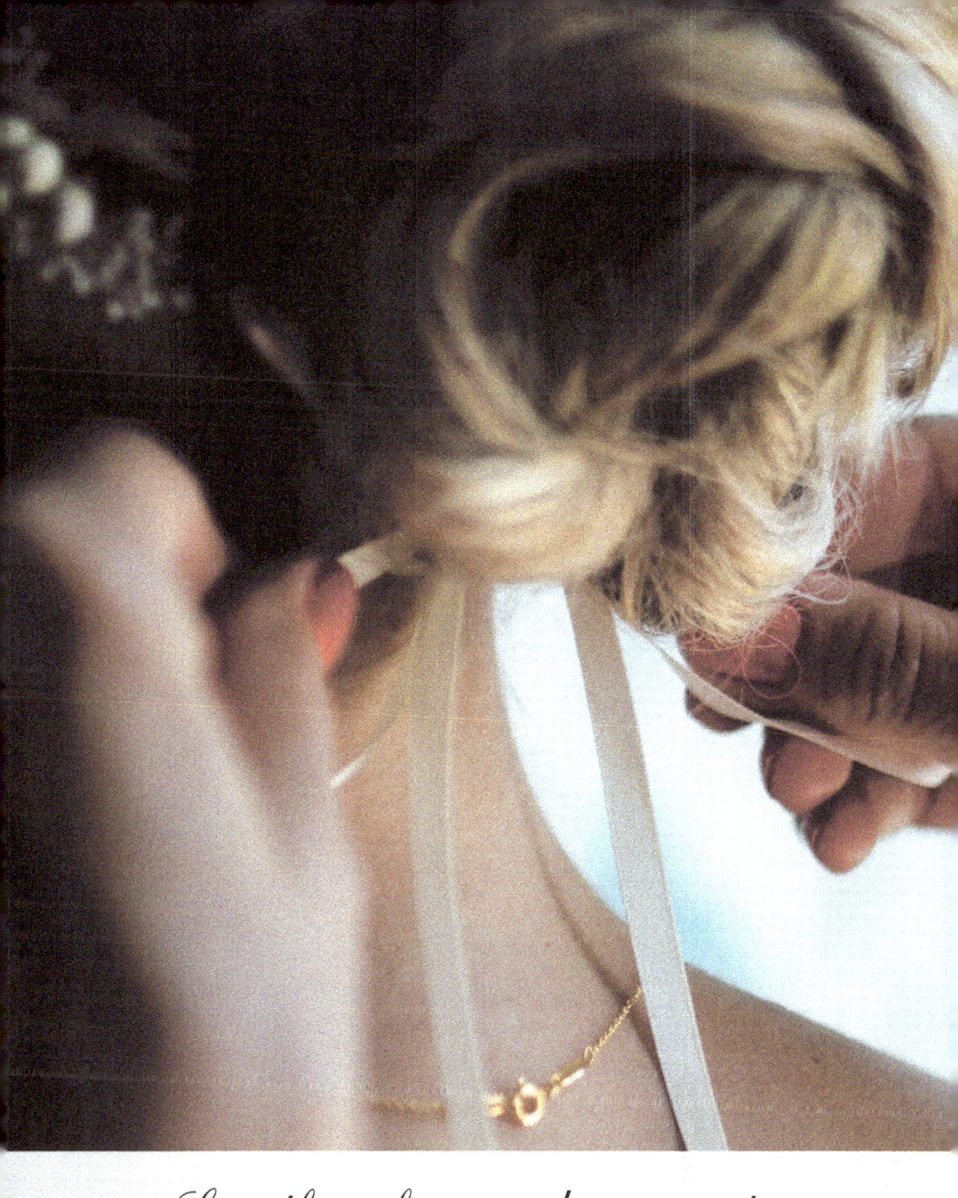

Something borrowed represents
the well-wishing of others.

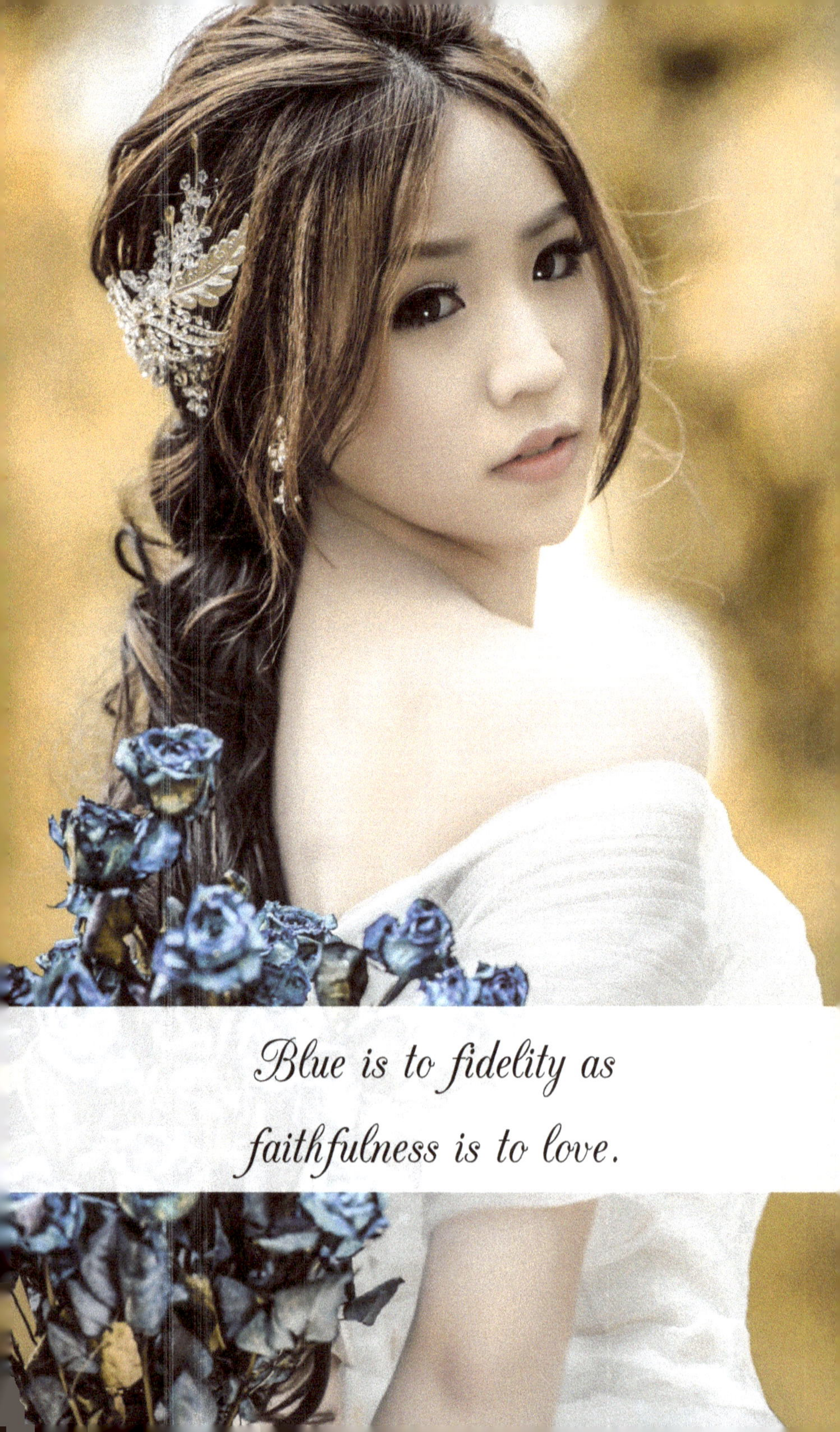

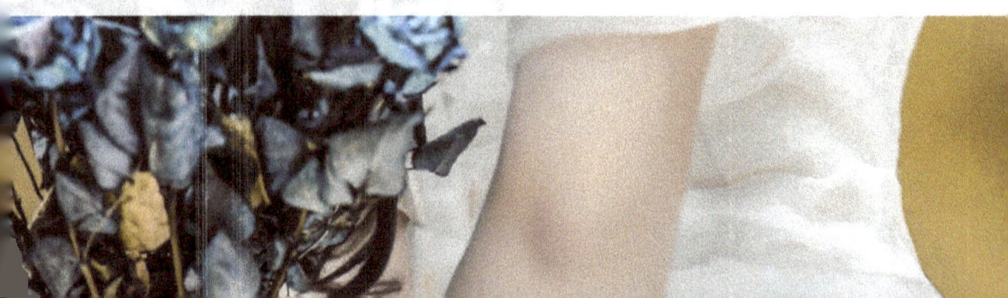

Blue is to fidelity as
faithfulness is to love.

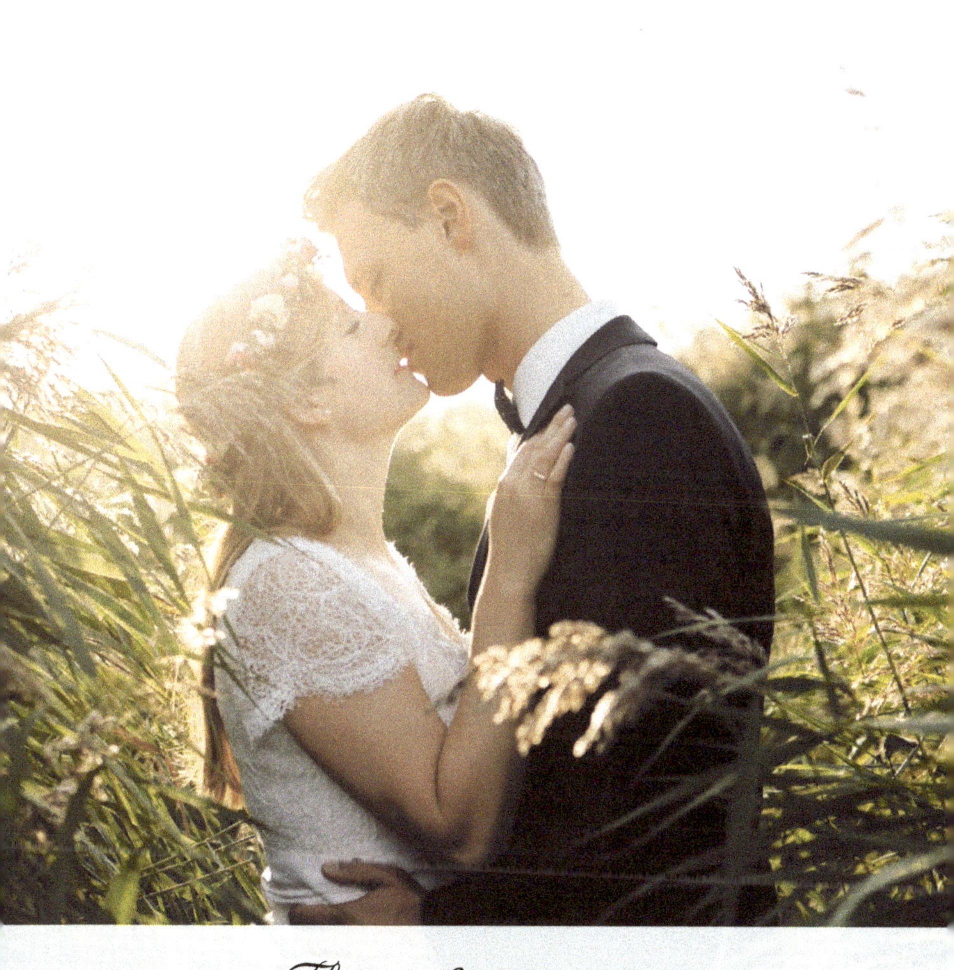

The perfect song is
sung within the heart.

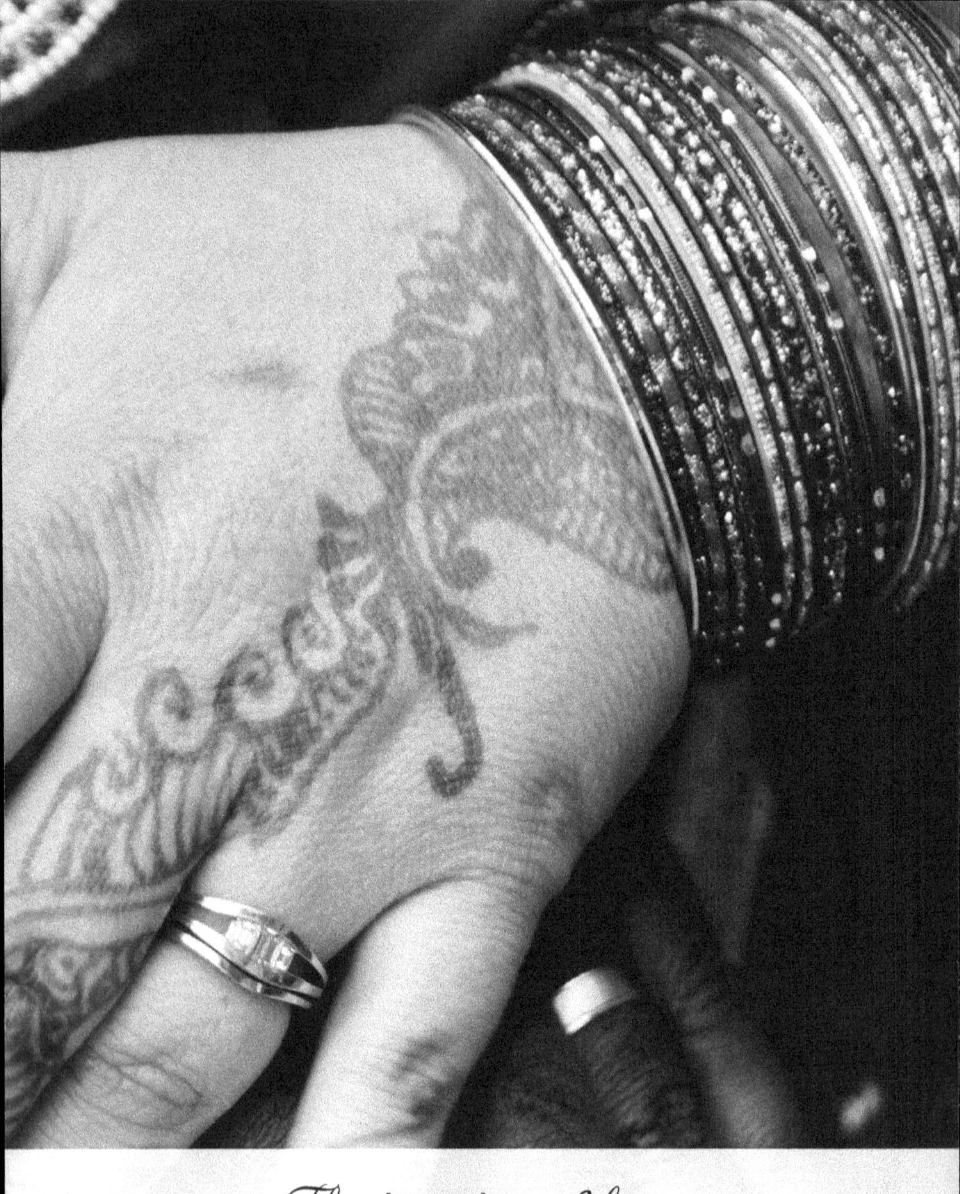

The tapestry of love is woven by four hands.

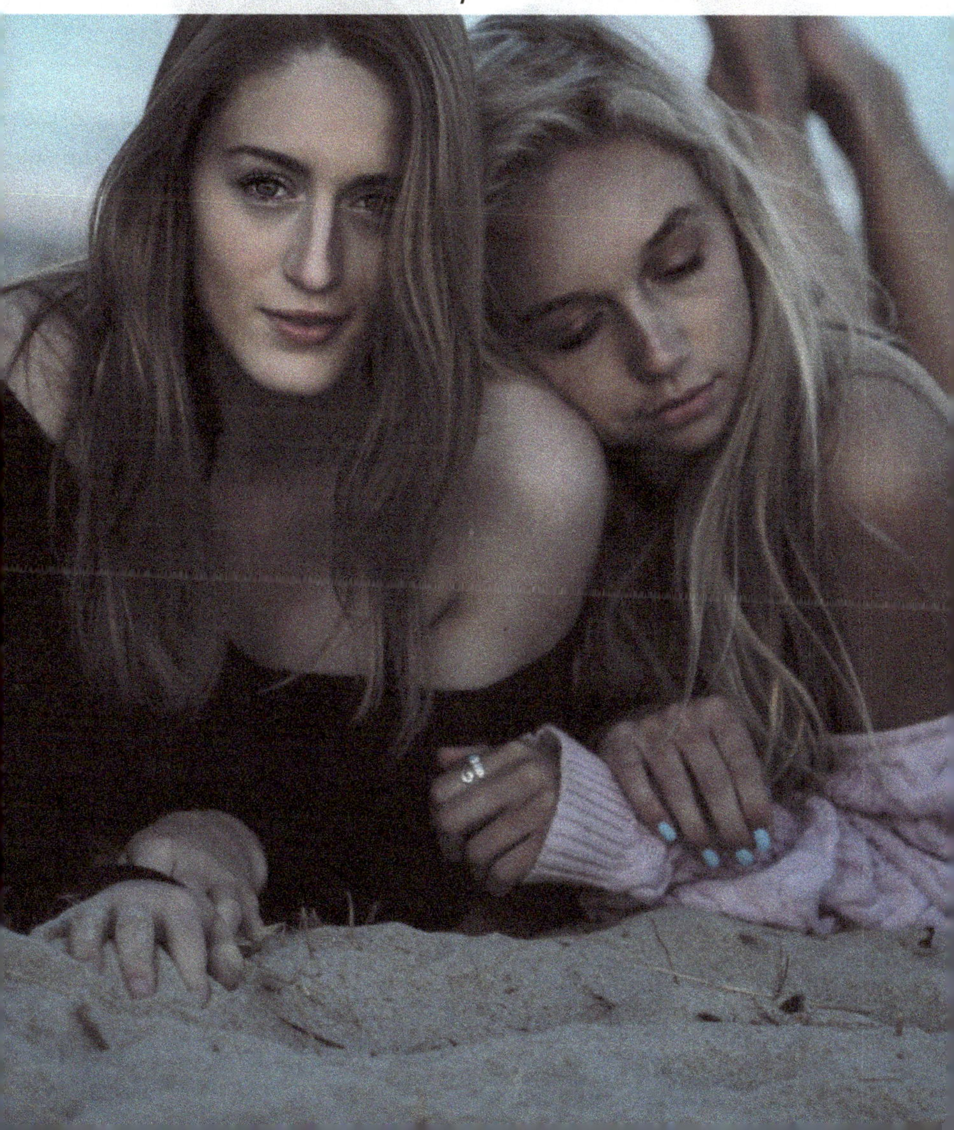


To take is to choose

with an open heart.

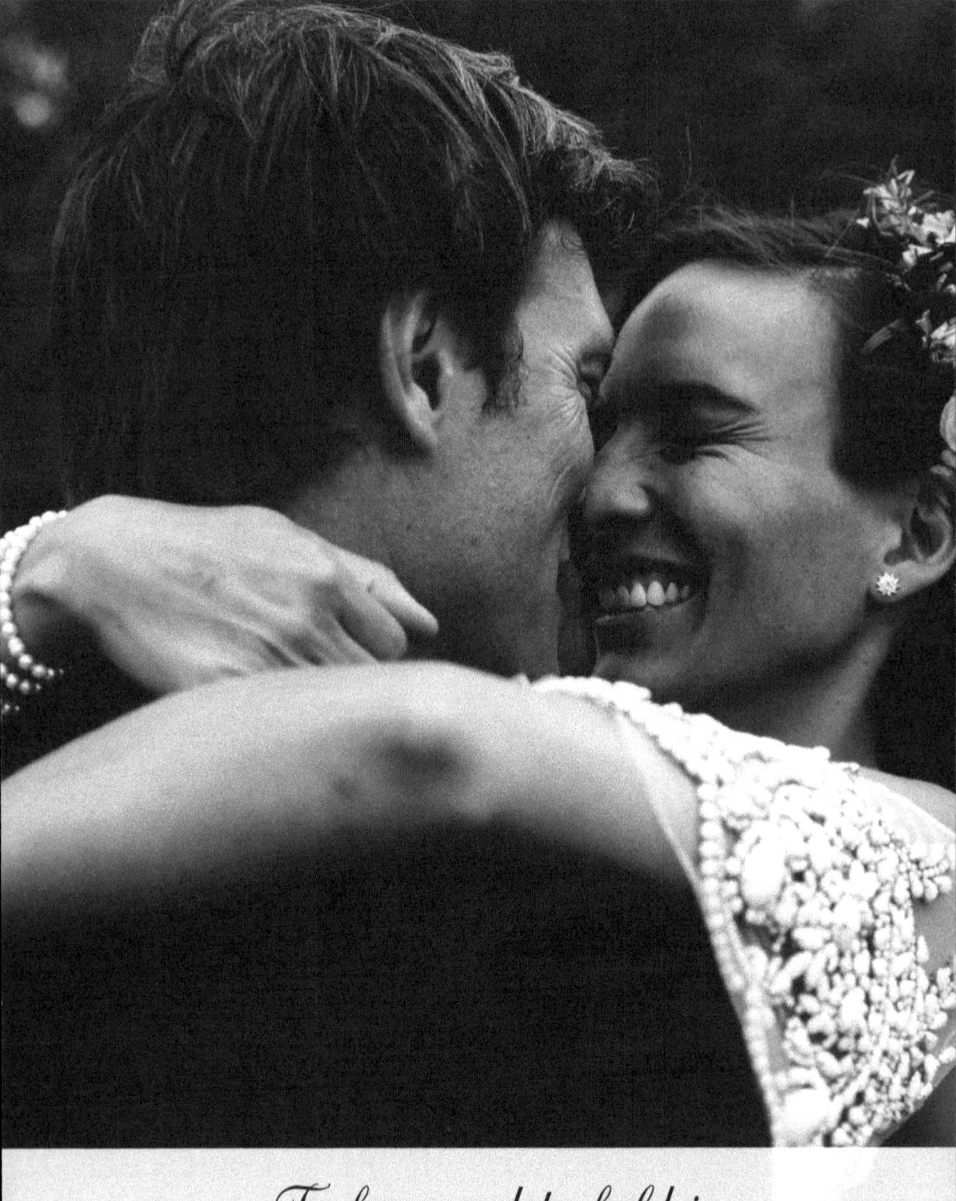
To have and to hold is
to receive and to treasure.

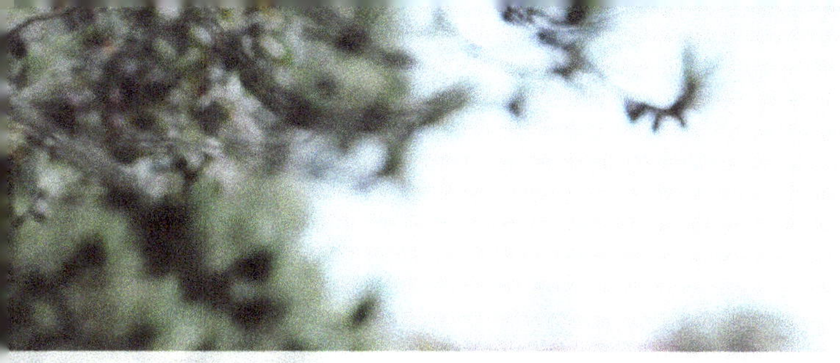
To cherish is
to love.

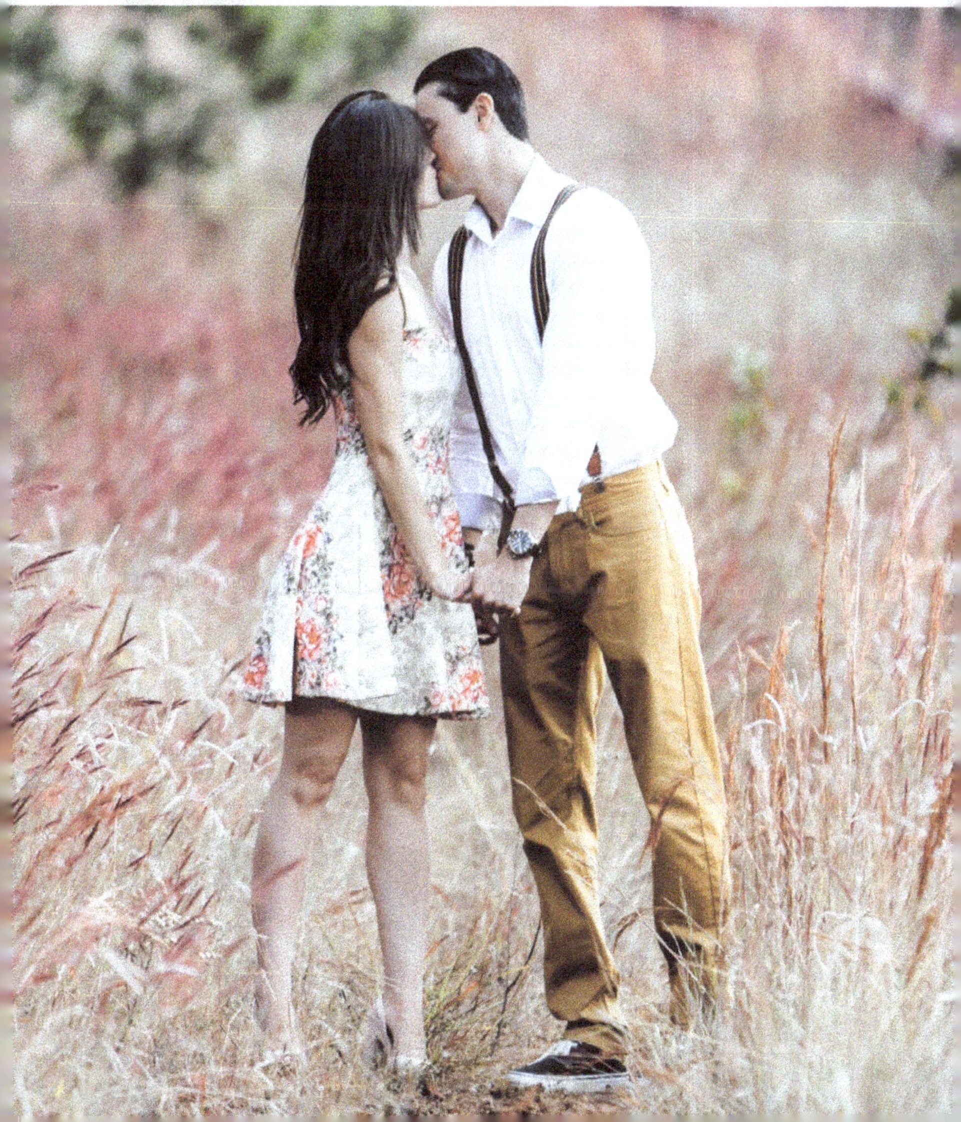

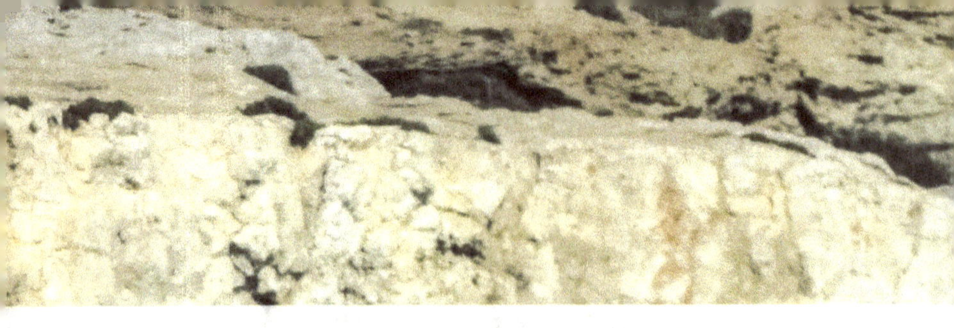


Richer or poorer tallies

the wealth within the soul.

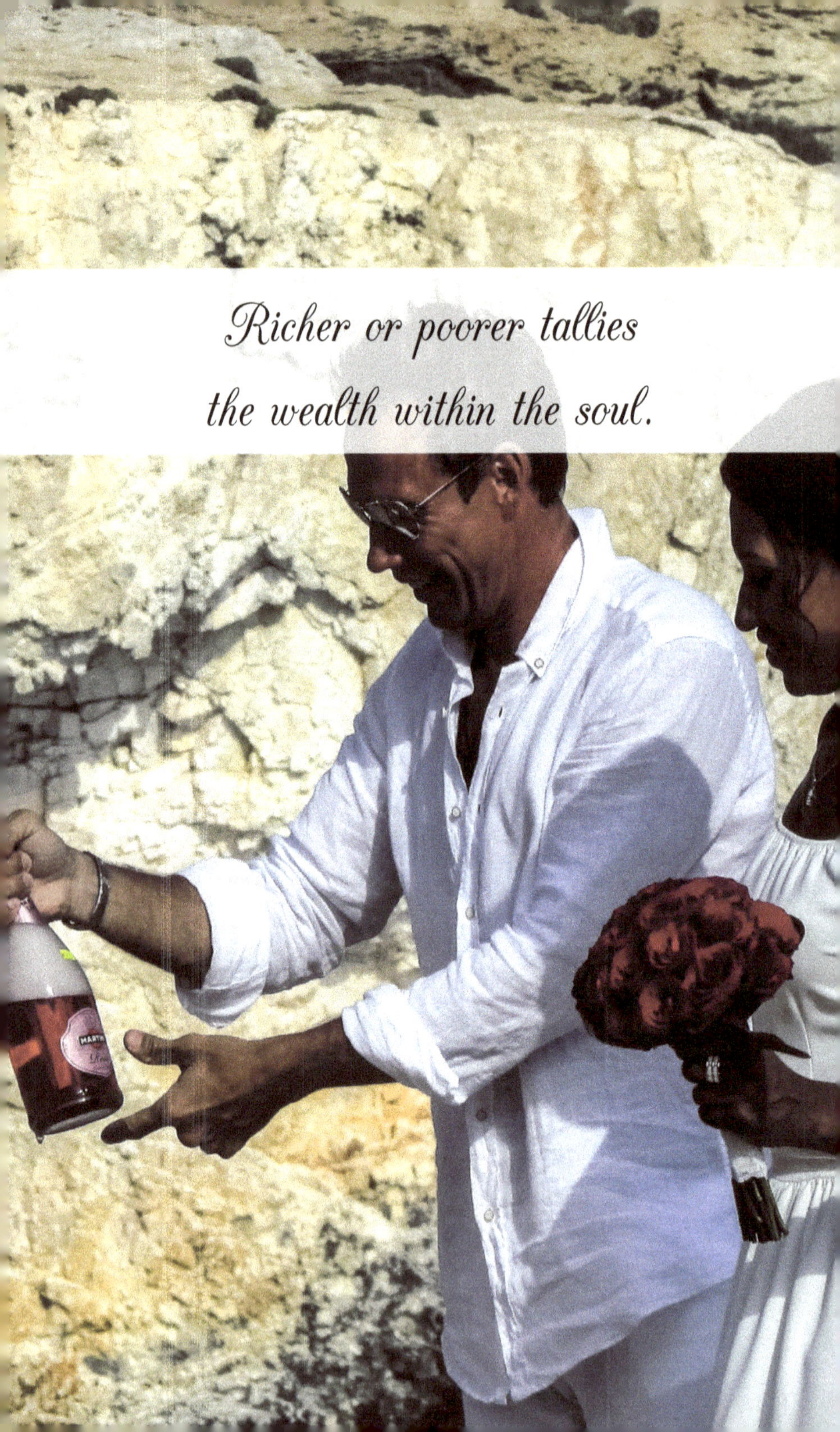

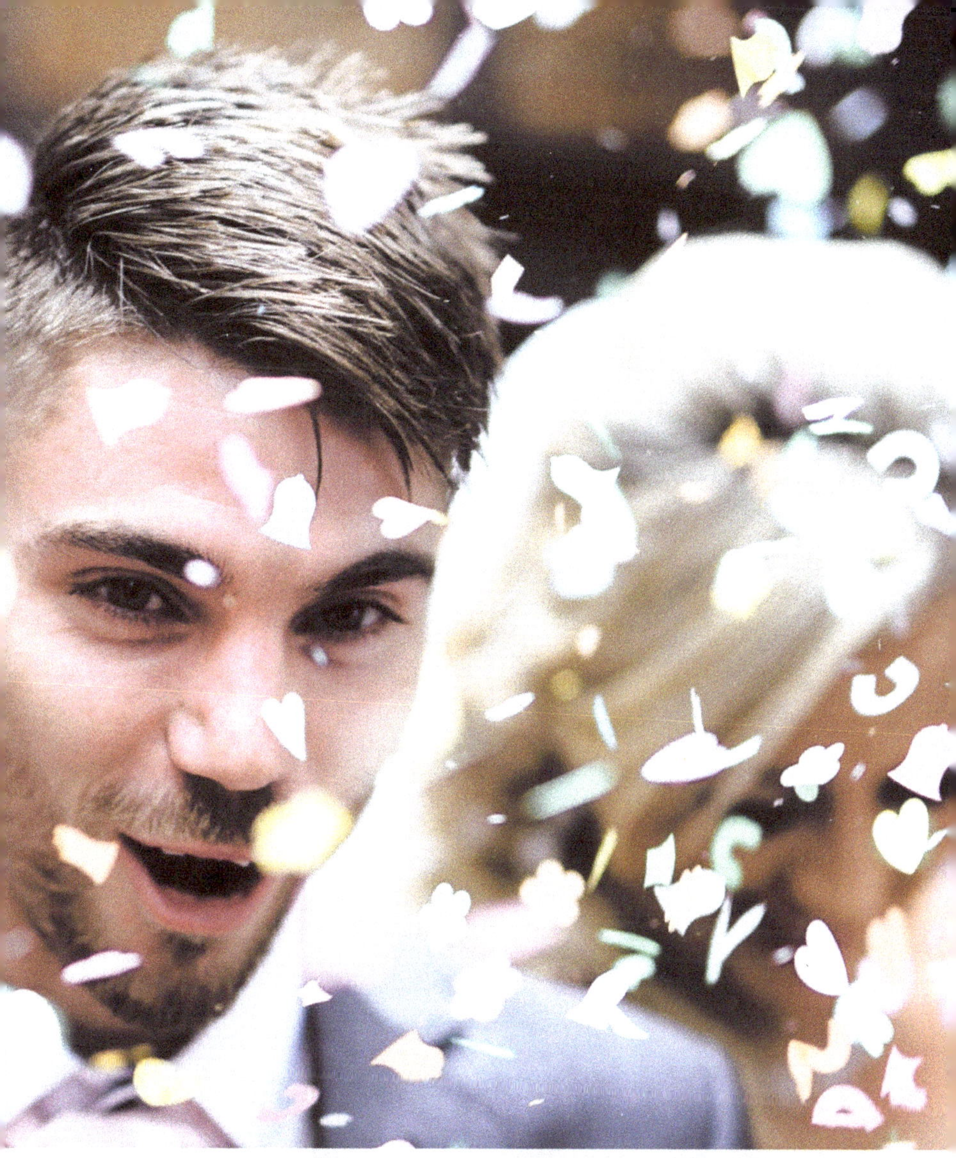

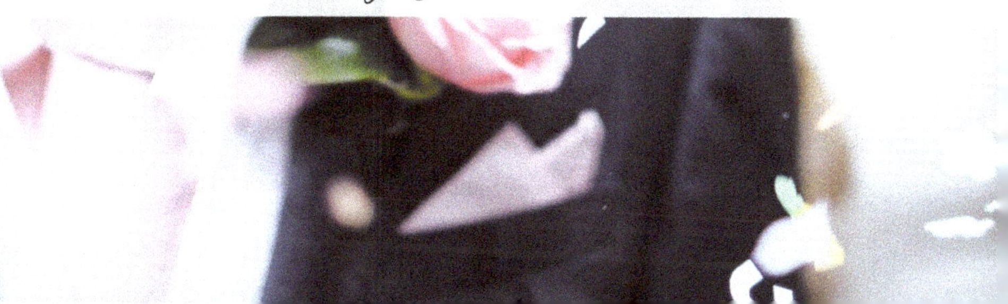

Obedience is demanded
only of the heart.

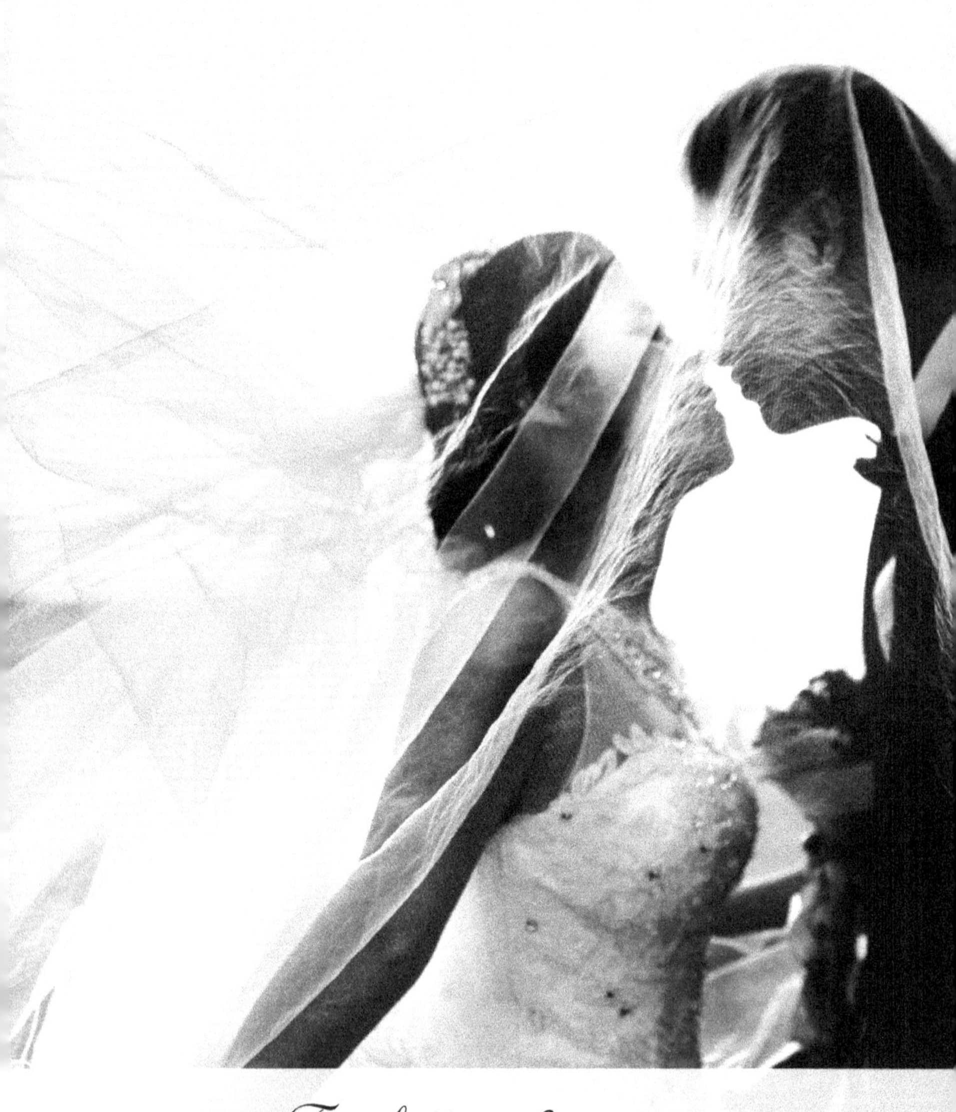

For better, for worse
puts the best first.

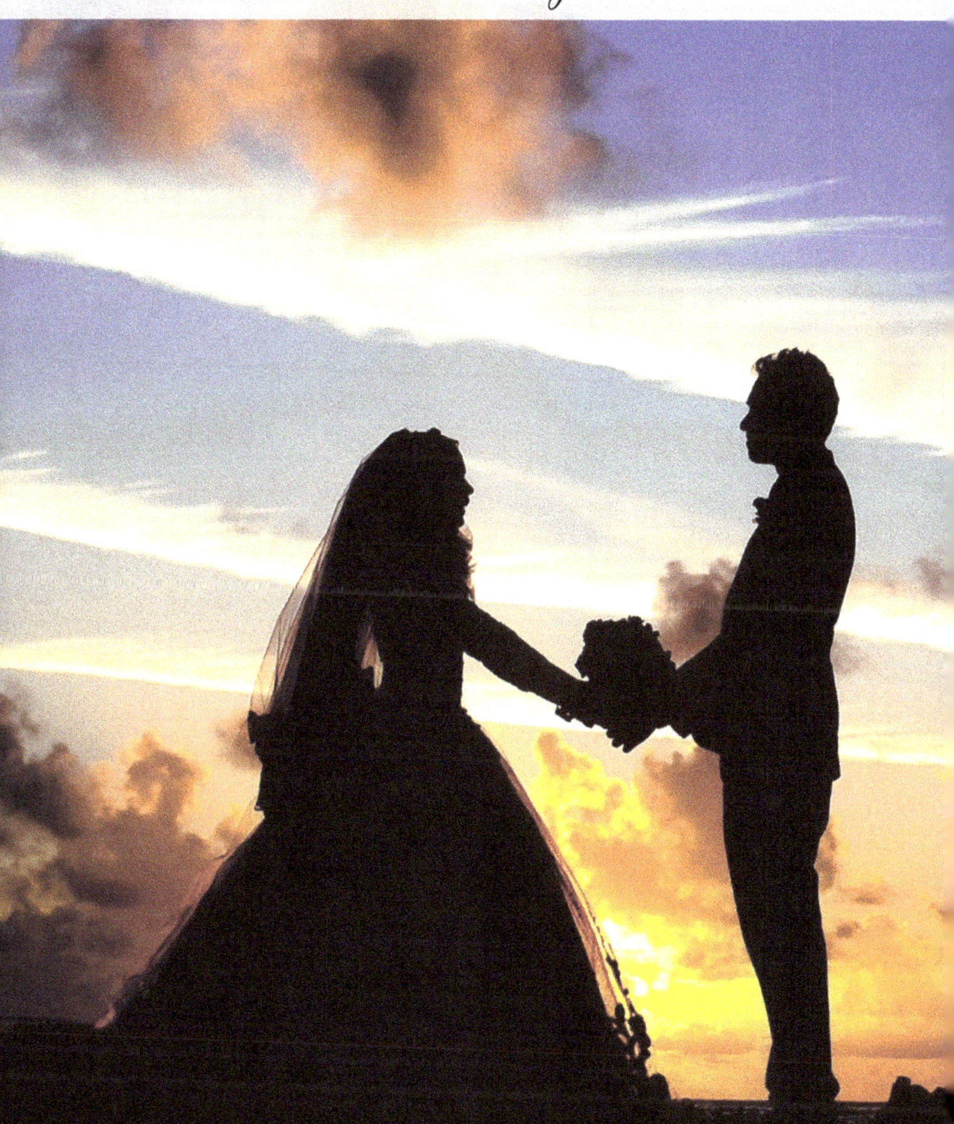

From this day forward
renews with every dawn.

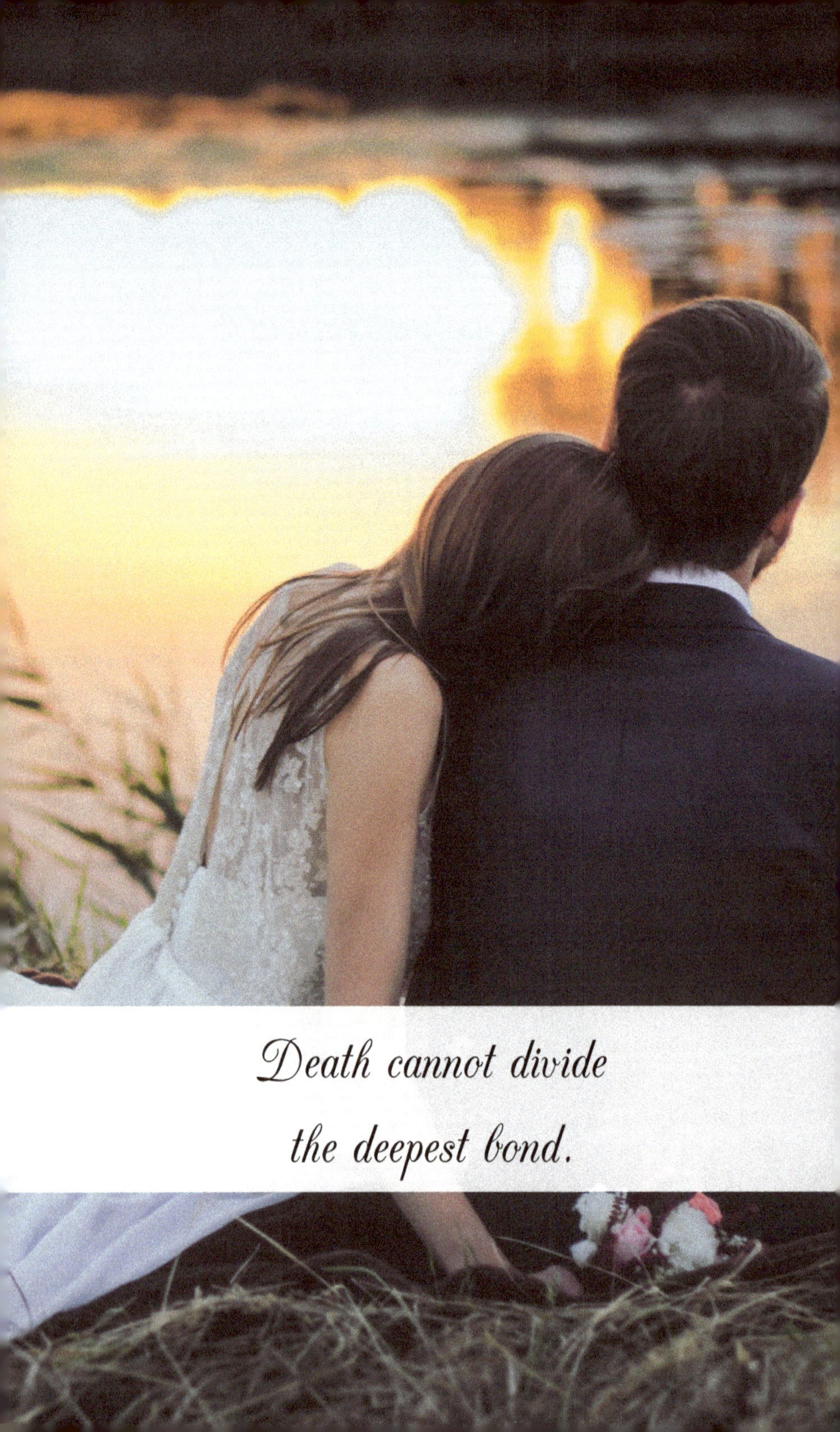

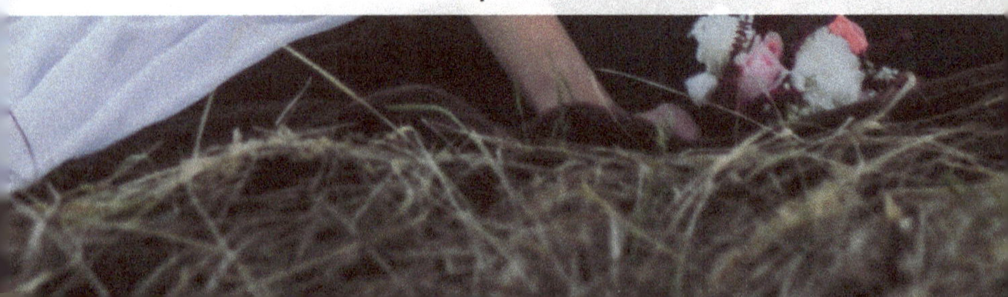
Death cannot divide
the deepest bond.

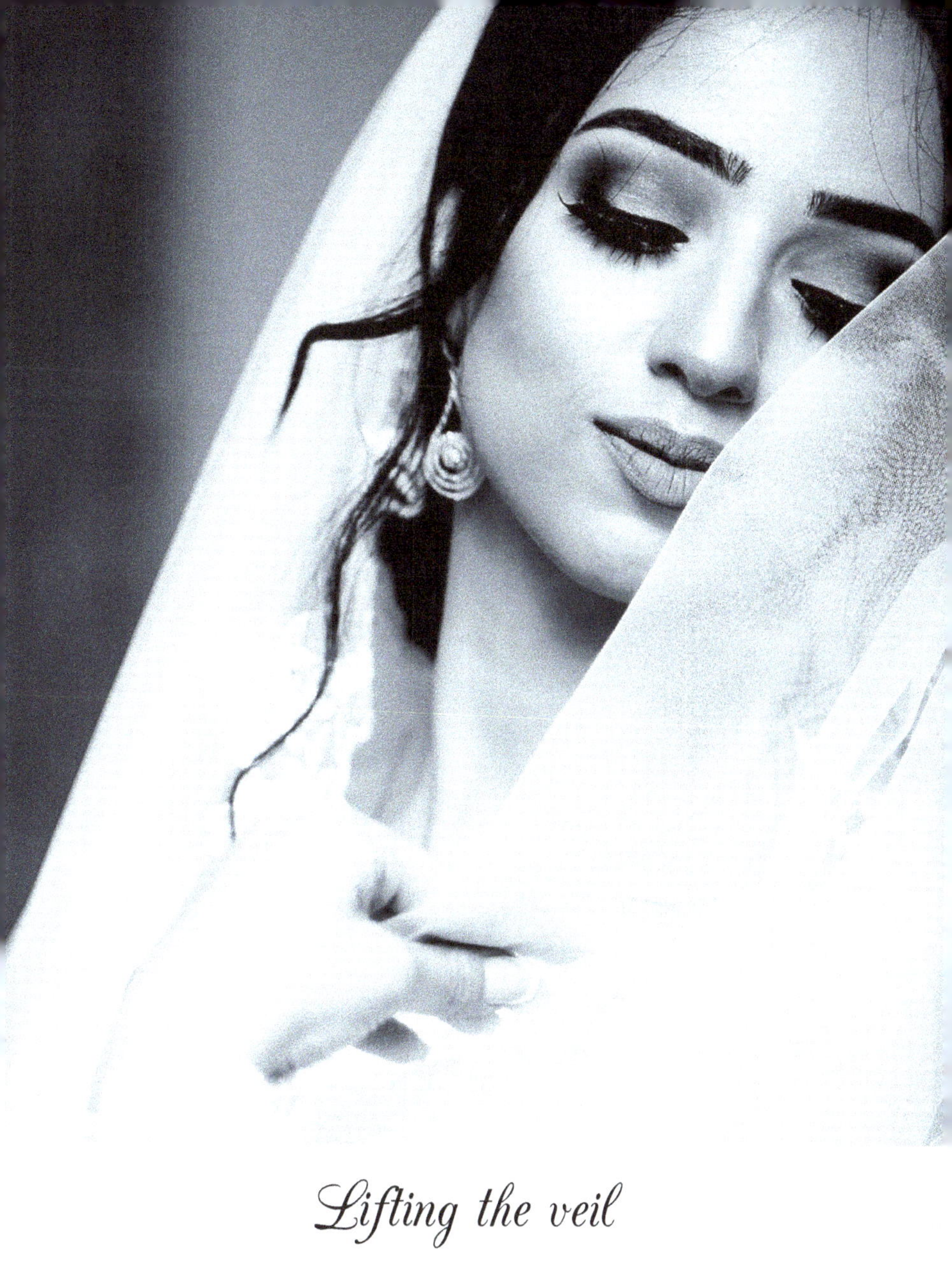

*Lifting the veil*

*is revelatory.*

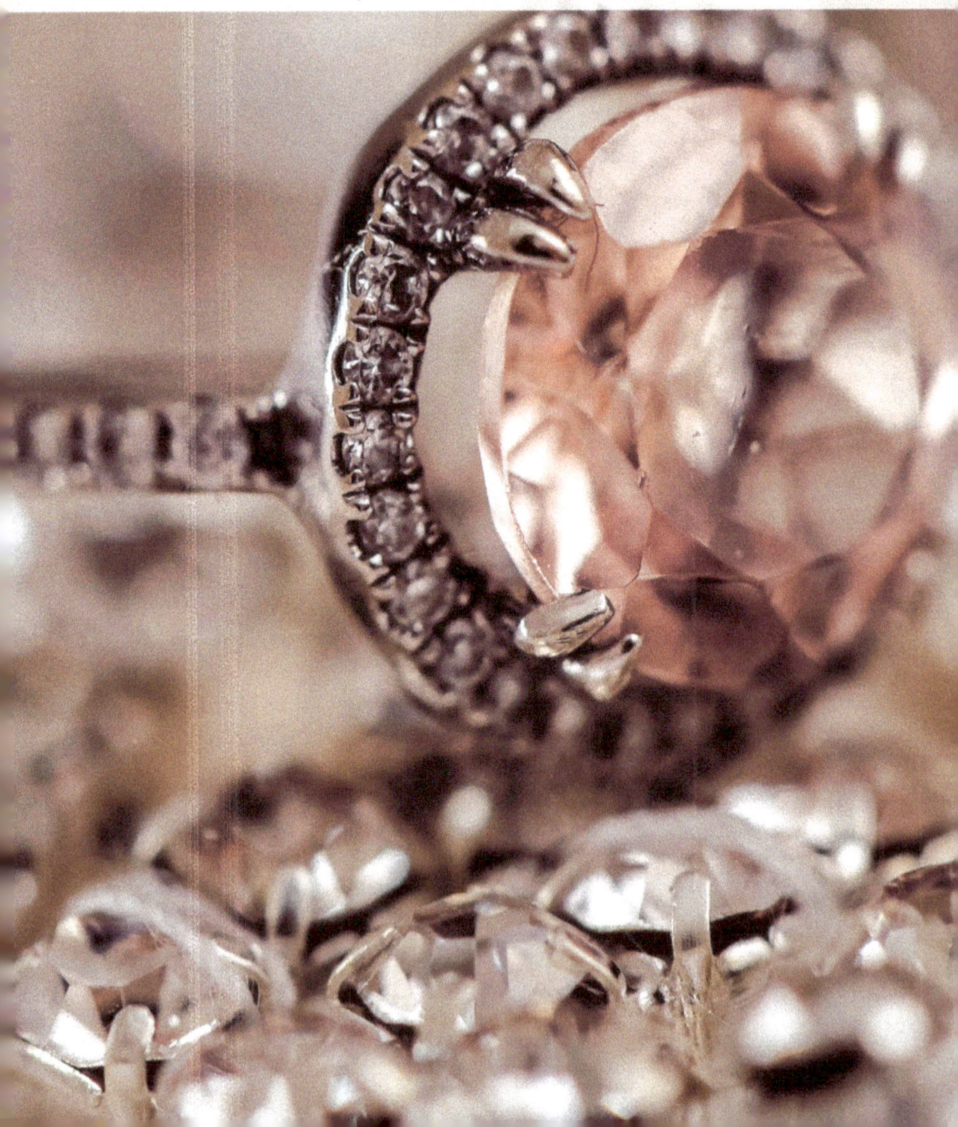

Diamonds aren't forever.
The promise is eternal.

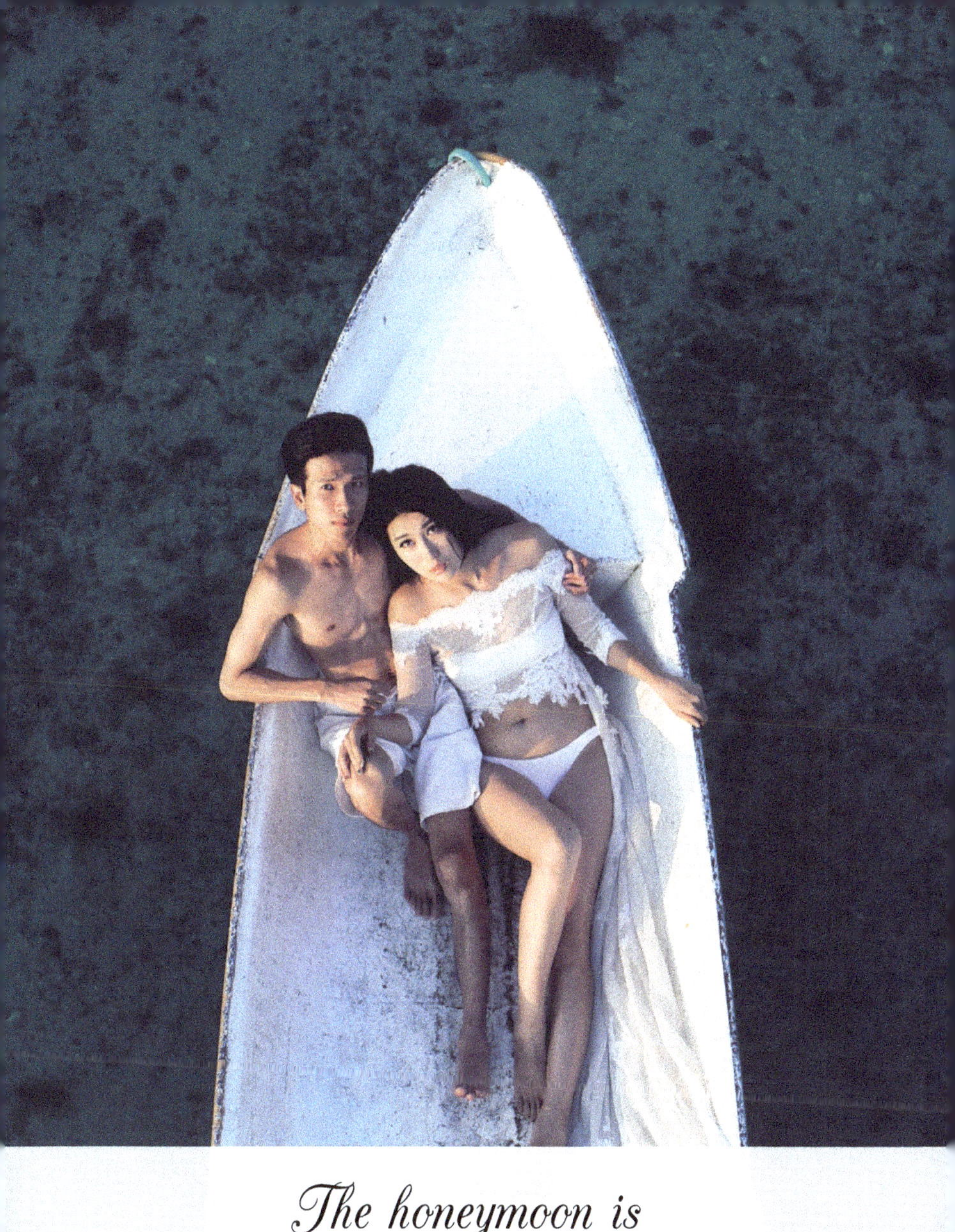

The honeymoon is
a time of transition.

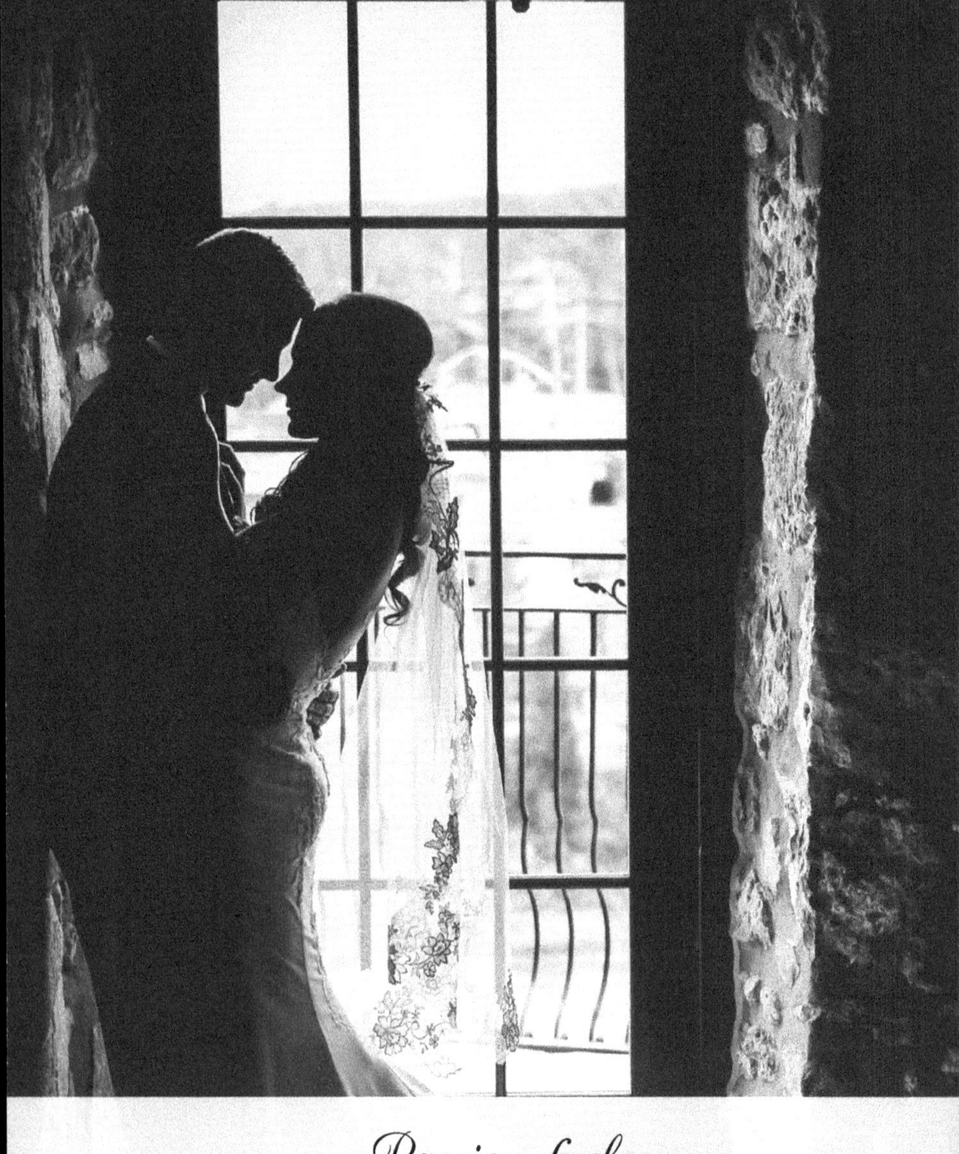

*Passion fuels*

*all pleasure.*

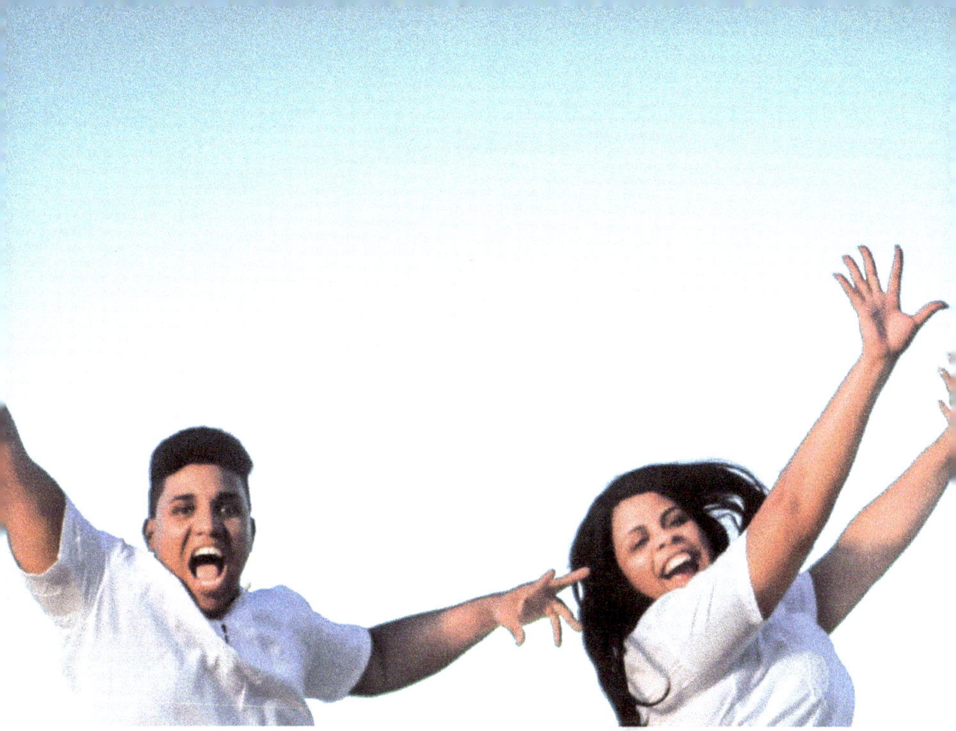

Marriage is the crucible

of transformation.

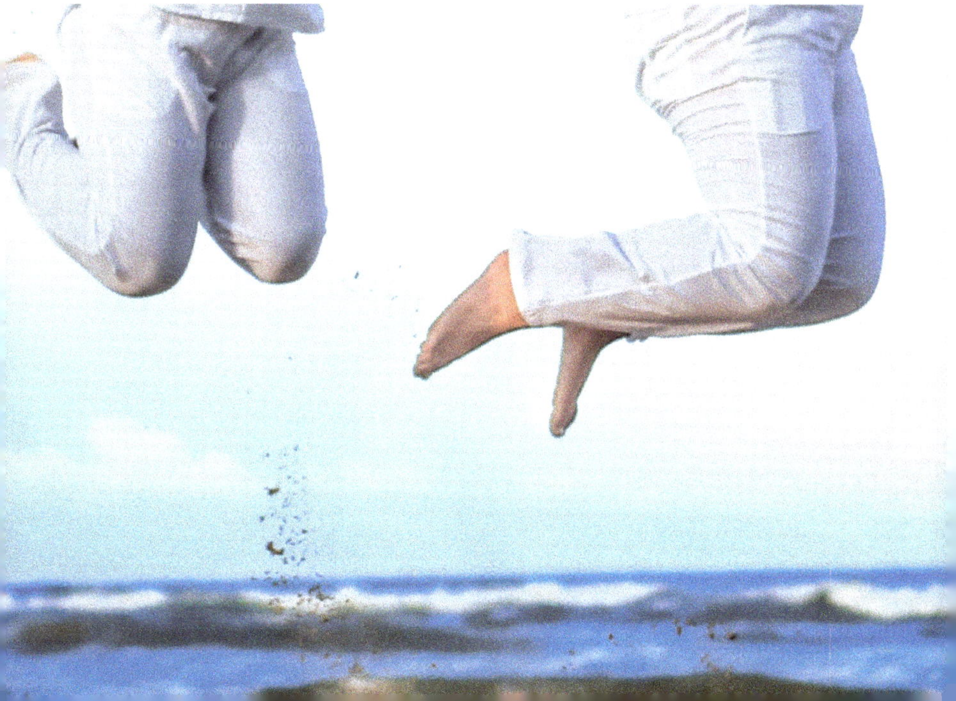

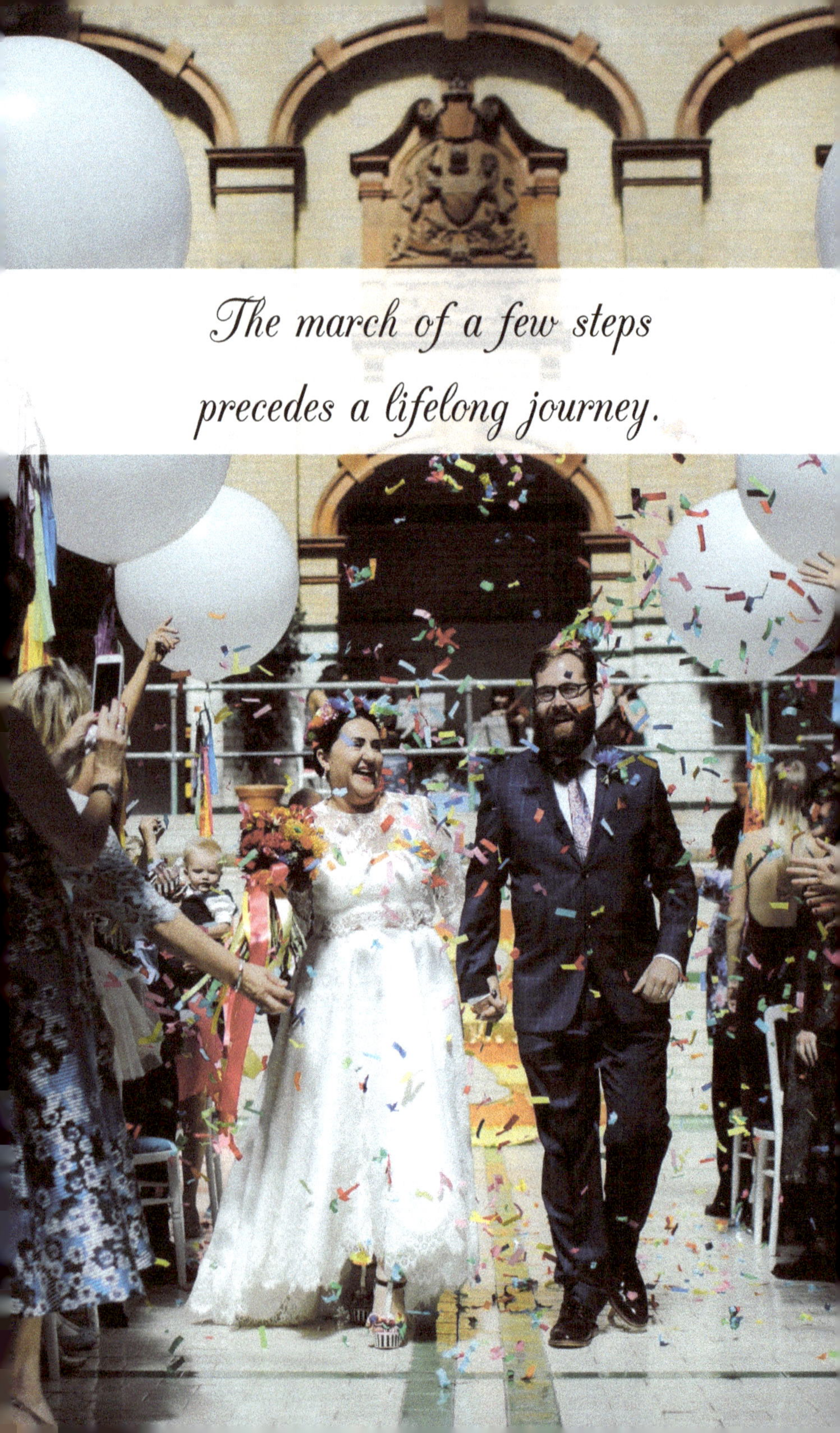

The march of a few steps
precedes a lifelong journey.

Once across the threshold,

each carries the other.

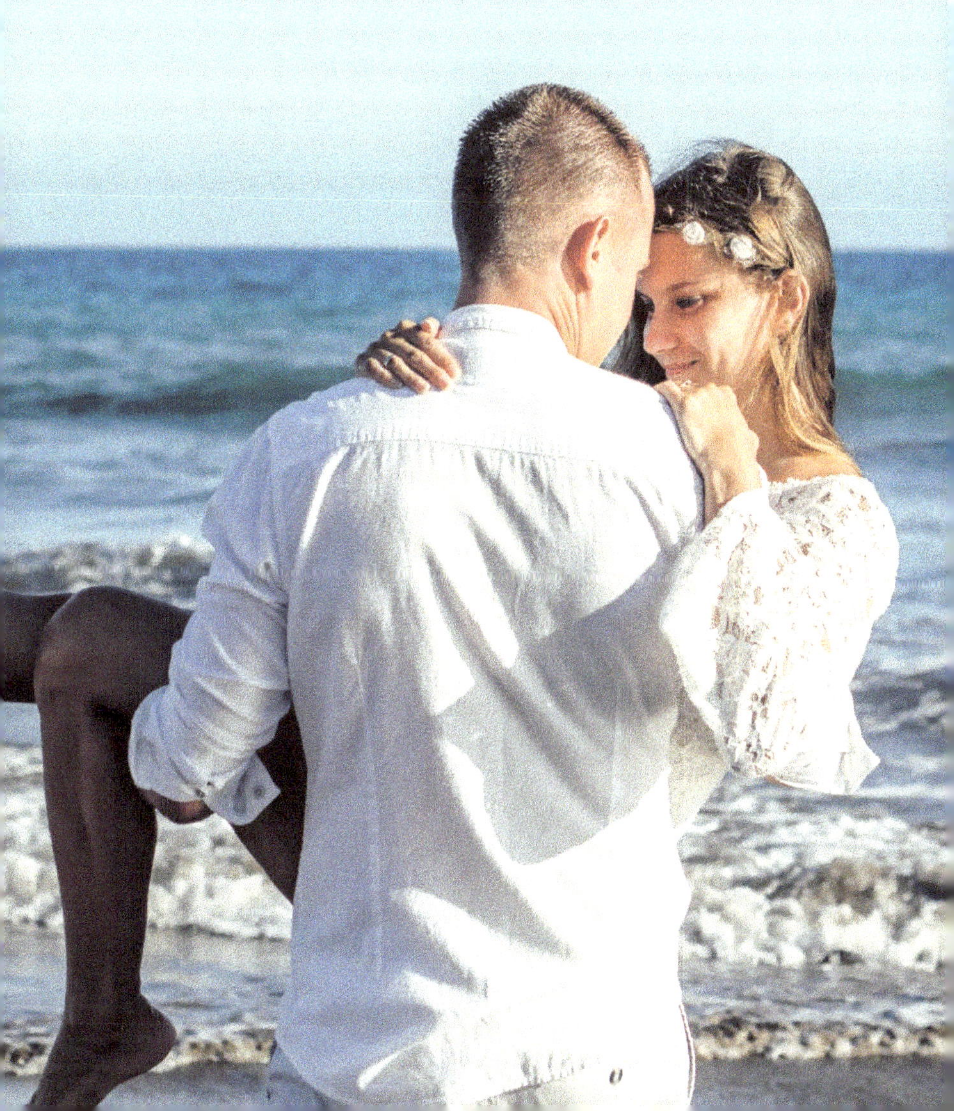

# About the Author

Laine Cunningham's books take readers on adventures around the world. *The Family Made of Dust* is set in the Australian Outback, while *Reparation* is a novel of the American Great Plains. Her women's travel adventure memoir *Woman Alone: A Six-Month Journey Through the Australian Outback* appeals to fans of *Wild* and *Eat Pray Love*. Her work has received multiple awards including the Hackney and the James Jones Fellowship, and has been published by *Reed, Birmingham Arts Journal*, and the annual anthology by *Writer's Digest*. She is the senior editor of *Sunspot Literary Journal*.

## Fiction

*The Family Made of Dust*
*Beloved*
*Reparation*

## Nonfiction

*Woman Alone*

*On the Wallaby Track: Australian Words and Phrases*

*Seven Sisters: Messages from Aboriginal Australia*

*Writing While Female or Black or Gay*

*The Wisdom of Puppies*
*The Wisdom of Babies*
*The Wisdom of Weddings*


*The Zen of Travel*
*The Zen of Gardening*
*Zen in the Stable*
*The Zen of Chocolate*
*The Zen of Dogs*

*Bikes of Berlin*
*Necropolises of New Orleans I & II*
*Ruins of Rome I & II*
*Ancients of Assisi I & II*
*Panoramas of Portugal*
*Nuances of New York*
*Glimpses of Germany*
*Impressions of Italy*
*Altitudes of the Alps*
*Knights Through the Ages*
*Utopia of the Unicorn*
*Portraits of Paris*
*Flourishes of France*